Praise for
Vessels: A Memoir of Borders

Between bodies and language. Between artist and survivor. Between aquí y allá. Straddling sacred spaces, Chicanx writer Michelle Otero claims deep roots in a mestiza landscape. Through memory, poems, dreams, and letters, *Vessels: A Memoir of Borders* is a mythical journey celebrating "Herencia" and "Ritual" as the presence of the past—her own as well as that of her ancestors. She evokes a deep sense of intentional healing while embracing and disrupting relationships. Recounting the vital lessons of her traumas with an open heart, she shapes a profound memoir as an offering for us to witness our own prayers.

—**Richard Yañez**, author of *El Paso del Norte: Stories on the Border*

"How does suffering yield such light?" This is among the driving questions of *Vessels: A Memoir of Borders*, a remarkable excavation of loss, abuse, trauma, dislocation, and the mysteries of grace and resilience. Part memory, part map, part poem, part prayer, *Vessels* reveals hard truths about the harms committed upon women and the legacies of silence and shame. In her quest to reassemble a broken identity, Otero channels Coyolxahqui, Malinche, and ancestral ghosts who guide her through a labyrinth of choices, regrets, joys and wisdoms echoing throughout generations. This book aims for the heart, with language that reaches, root-like, and images that cut and shine. Ultimately, *Vessels* is a journey of reclamation – of returning to oneself, to earth that sustains, to culture that endures, to those who 'love back to wholeness.' A stunning literary mosaic."

—**Harrison Candelaria Fletcher**, author of *Finding Querencia: Essays from In-Between*

I can't imagine the courage it took for Michelle Otero to tell this story but lucky for us, she did. Here is suffering transformed into power, the power of a woman who against all odds finds her voice...and the key to healing. What a gift! Readers will not be able to put this book down.

—**Demetria Martinez**

Michelle Otero is a gifted writer, and this memoir is rich and fascinating. I was deeply moved by it.

—**Luis Alberto Urrea,** author of *Piedra* and *Goodnight, Irene*

VESSELS:
A Memoir of Borders

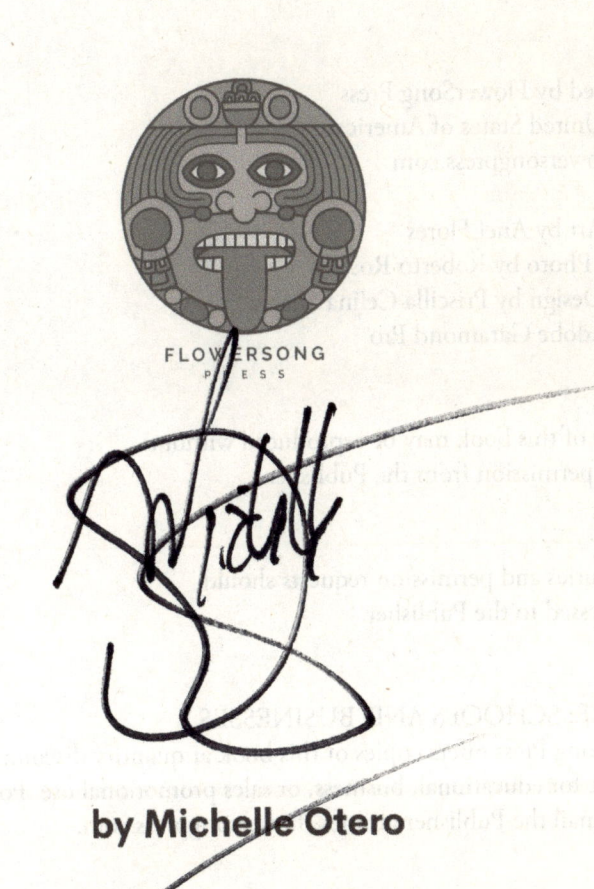

FLOWERSONG
PRESS

by Michelle Otero

FLOWERSONG
PRESS

FlowerSong Press
Copyright © 2023 by Michelle Otero
ISBN: 978-1-953447-86-9
Library of Congress Control Number: 2023932962

Published by FlowerSong Press
in the United States of America.
www.flowersongpress.com

Cover Art by Anel Flores
Author Photo by Roberto Rosales
Cover Design by Priscilla Celina Suarez
Set in Adobe Garamond Pro

No part of this book may be reproduced without written permission from the Publisher.

All inquiries and permission requests should be addressed to the Publisher.

NOTICE: SCHOOLS AND BUSINESSES
FlowerSong Press offers copies of this book at quantity discount with bulk purchase for educational, business, or sales promotional use. For information, please email the Publisher at info@flowersongpress.com.

Para mi abuelo materno, Florentino Moran.

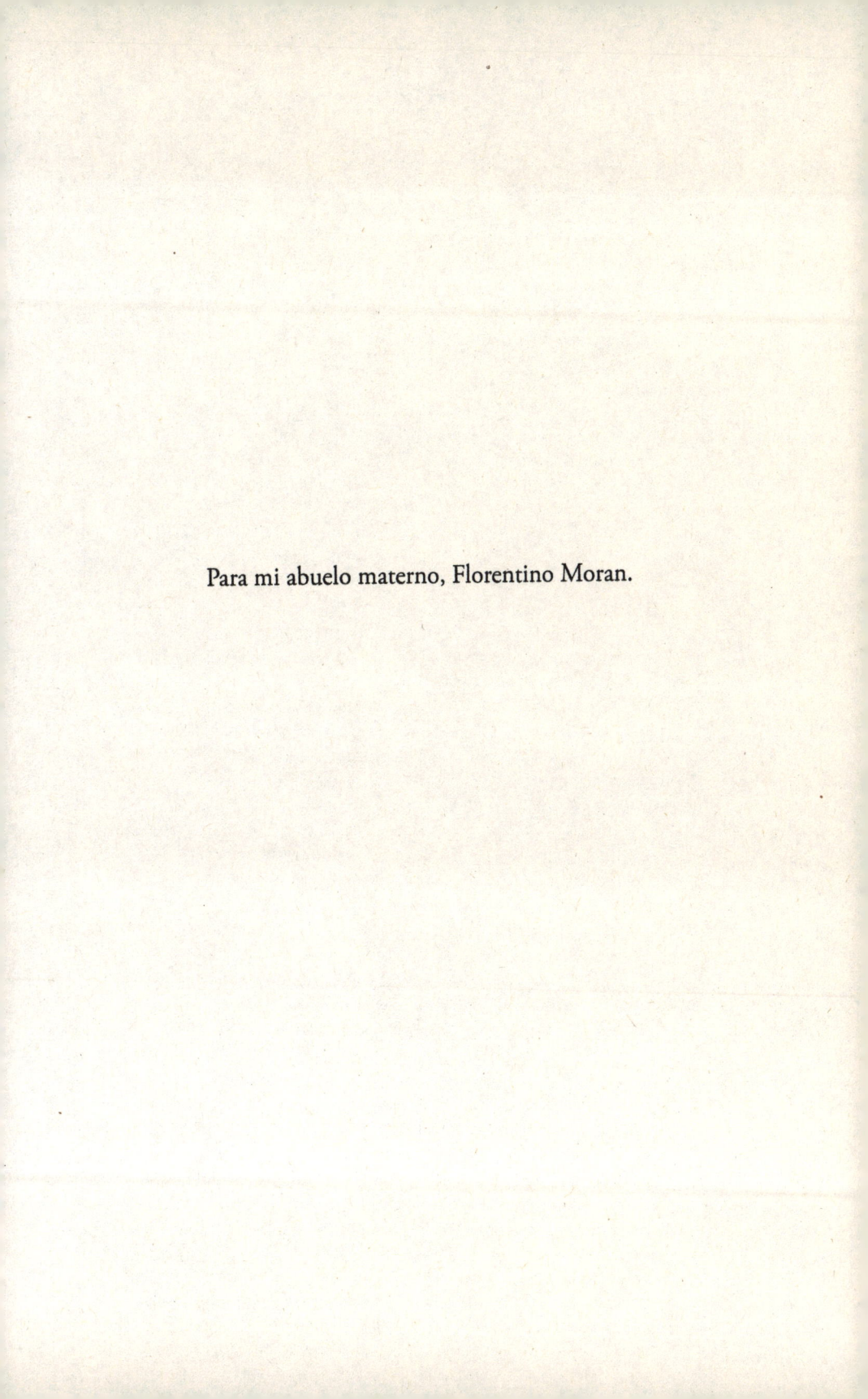

Para mi abuelo materno, Florentino Morán.

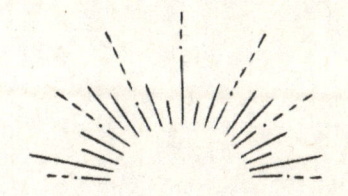

Table of Contents

Author's Note......ix

Prologue......3

East / Tlahuitzlampa......7

West / Cihuatlampa......39

North / Mictlampa......93

South / Huitzlampa......139

Sky......195

Earth......217

El Ombligo......231

Notes......239

Acknowledgements......240

About the Author......243

Author's Note

This vessel is constructed of my memories and my truth. My memories and truth might differ from those of the people who shared these moments with me.

In some instances, my memories and truth come from dreams or imaginings of things I could not have experienced. I never met my great-grandparents or Malinche frente a frente. I wrote them into this story because I had a deep need to know them, and the threads connecting me to them were faint as daddy long leg webs. I know where some of my ancestors died but not where they were born. I know that an Irish man named Moran got together with a woman whose name is lost to my family in San Luís Potosí, and from their union came my Great-Grandfather Crecencio. I've seen and read the composites sketched of La Malinche, but I don't know what she might have said about her own life. From these threads I've tried to weave a story that connects to my own life. Writing this story has helped me to know them, helped me to take my place in their lineage.

In some instances, I have compressed scenes for brevity and the sake of story.

In some instances, I have created composite characters to protect individual privacy.

Cómo dice el dicho, Cada cabeza es un mundo.

"Coyolxauhqui appears in your life when you feel broken into pieces."

–Jade Oracle

"The Coyolxauhqui Imperative is to heal and achieve integration...The Coyolxauhqui Imperative is an ongoing process of making and unmaking."

–Gloria Anzaldúa

VESSELS:
A Memoir of Borders

Prologue

Variations on the Death of Coyolxauhqui

Coyolxauhqui—bells her
cheeks, breasts
hang down. Mother.

I
Her son Huitzilopochtli grew restless and wanted to leave their home, Coatepetl, or Snake Mountain. Coyolxauhqui wanted to stay.

My impulse was always to leave, to find a place far from home and make a home there, with new people, new stories, to reset, to get it right this time. Wigglesworth G-31. 19 Partridge Street, Belize City. 1140½ 11th Street Northwest. A guest-room in my brother and sister-in-law's house in El Paso. Corner of Cliff and Stanton, an 18-minute walk to my first creative writing class at UT El Paso. Back in my childhood bedroom in Deming. Grandma and Grandpa's spare room. Casa de huéspedes, Mártires de Tacubaya, Oaxaca, Centro. A house on a hill in Lachigoló. I flirted with a lover's terreno on the outskirts of Oaxaca, a writer's house in San Antonio, a widowed friend's empty room in Manhattan. I came back to New Mexico. I borrowed a friend's Old Town casita in Albuquerque, house-sat for a golfer in Algodones, and then signed a lease on my own downtown apartment with high ceilings and wood floors.

Huitzilopochtli cut off her head and ate her heart. Then he led the Mexica to Tenochtitlán.

Coyolxauhqui wanted to stay. My apartment—the entire building—died by fire. The Mexica found a home. Was there no other way?

II
As Coatlicue, mother of Coyolxauhqui and the four-hundred Centzon Huitznaua, cleaned the shrine atop Snake Mountain, a ball of feathers descended from the sky. She tucked the feathers in her belt and became

Prologue | 3

impregnated. Infuriated by their mother's pregnancy, Coyolxauhqui and her Huitznaua brothers set out to kill her.

I have four brothers. The last came when I was ten years old and the baby of the family, the only girl. My parents divorced when he was an infant. They remarried when he was four.

One brother warned Huitzilopochtli, the child in Coatlicue's womb, of the impending attack. Huitzilopochtli sprang from his mother fully grown and armed with the xiuhcoatl, a ray of sun. He butchered his brothers and cast them into the southern sky, where they became the stars. He dismembered Coyolxauhqui and cut off her head. He tossed her limbs and torso to the foot of Coatepetl and cast her head into the sky, where she became the moon.

How does suffering yield such light?

III
Coyolxauhqui cut off her mother's head. Huitzilopochtli, the child in Coatlicue's womb, sprang from her neck, fully grown and fully armed. He dismembered Coyolxauhqui and cut off her head. He tossed her limbs and torso to the foot of Coatepetl and cast her head into the sky, where she became the moon.

Brother born fully armed. Daughter killed protecting her home.

IV
When Coyolxauhqui and her brothers arrived at Coatepec, Coatlicue had already given birth to Huitzilopochtli. He decapitated his sister and brothers. He tossed their bodies to the foot of Coatepetl and cast their heads into the sky, where Coyolxauhqui became the moon and the 400 brothers became the stars.

Huitzilopochtli, as the sun, overcomes the stars and moon.

Or Huitzilopochtli is the sun, and Coyolxauhqui is the Milky Way.

Or the patriarchy destroys the feminine.[1]

*

From the womb, he tells his mother, "Do not be afraid, I know what I must do."

*

He was born fully armed.

She was the only daughter.

*

She appears in a circular stone, her limbs jagged, bone exposed. Scallop shapes at the neck and limbs indicate she was dismembered and decapitated. Femur bones protrude from her severed legs.

How does a woman fit in a stone?

How does a woman fit in a circle?

What is my frame? How do I twist, turn, bend, break my body to fit?

*

A carved stone disk was found at the base of the Templo Mayor on the Huitzilopochtli side. Sacrificial victims stepped across her on their way to death. Priests rolled their bodies down the temple steps.

*

Her head carved in greenstone during the reign of Ahuitzotl sits at the Museum of Anthropology in Mexico City.

---

1 This telling of the Coyolxauhqui story is modified from *Jade Oracle*, co-created by Veronica Iglesias, Anne Key, and Ramona Snow Teo.

*

Coyolli—small metal bells.
Warrior.

Coyolxauhqui—strings of bells
around her calves. Warrior.

*

Carved in nine ton
stone one
foot thick.

Coyolxauhqui. Broken woman.

*

Sometimes babies break us. Sometimes it's men we love. Sometimes it's both.

*

The gods of our ancestors don't fuck around. Coatlicue, claw-feet Mother, wore a skirt of intertwined serpents and a necklace of human hands and hearts. Daughter Coyolxauhqui's severed head became the moon. Huitzilopochtli was born fully formed, fully armed, a ray of lightning in his hand.

My grandma smoked Kent III 100's and picked our pimples with blunt fingernails.

In Mexico, Jesus weeps.

*

We are all Coyolxauhqui. We who defend our home. We who say the hard thing. We who warn. We who won't be taken. We who disagree, who see, who speak truth. How do we put ourselves back together?

East / Tlahuitzlampa

rumbo de la luz, rumbo del aprendizaje
rumbo donde sale el sol

Remedio
almost winter—before

"Mi'ja, did I ever tell you why I got so sick?" Grandpa Tino asked as I drove him an hour east from Deming to the bigger hospital, with its lung specialist and oncology department, in Las Cruces. My grandma was in critical care again, this time with pneumonia, after too short a recovery from having a lung removed a month and a half earlier. Grandpa and I were on that stretch of Interstate 10 between mountains, where the rocky Floridas slipped from view and the Organs had yet to reveal their jagged peaks.

"No," I said quietly. Mesquite and chamisa blurred past his window. I thought of cottontails sheltering beneath the low canopy, how they respond to threat, how my whole life I'd wanted them to relax on my approach, to know I come in peace, to eat from my hand and let me hold them. But, always, they scattered with my slightest movement. Gentle, gentle. I said, "No Grandpa, you never did."

*

By the time we reach the hospital, a nurse is giving Grandma a sponge bath, and the lung specialist has already made his rounds, so not only do we have to wait to see her, we can't ask the doctor how long she'll be here, how she got pneumonia, what this means for her cancer, how to pace ourselves, to parcel out our energy and hope. In the hall outside her room, Grandpa thrusts his flip phone into my hands, begging, "Call El Psychiatrist, mi'ja. Tell him your grandma is sick again. Tell him I need to see him."

*

El Psychiatrist leaves for vacation tomorrow, so Grandpa is squeezed into a thirty-minute slot between two regular appointments. We're a five-minute drive from the hospital where Grandma must have finished her sponge

East / Tlahuitzlampa | 9

bath and is probably eating lunch. She'll be tired when we get back. We won't have much time with her before she takes a nap.

"Tengo miedo," Grandpa says, sounding like a boy who's woken from a nightmare. He sits on a black leather armchair in the corner of his psychiatrist's office. The doctor sits across from him behind a cherry desk the size of my grandmother's hospital bed. He writes with a fountain pen in what must be Grandpa's file: *Florentino "Tino" Moran. 80 years old. World War II veteran. Spouse: Genevieve "China" Moran. 5 children. 16 grandchildren. Born 1923, Dolores, TX. Residence: Deming, NM. Occupation: Retired mechanic. Full disability. PTSD. Depression. Anxiety.*

Grandpa's hands clasp on his lap and then unclasp and touch down on the armrests, then his knees and thighs, smoothing the charcoal khakis I ironed for him this morning. His hands are the color of moist adobe, his veins like the roots of young desert willows, threaded beneath the surface in search of water, life.

I sit on a loveseat along the same wall as my grandpa's chair, his tweed hat and windbreaker next to me. He casts these items toward me no matter where we go—the hospital, doctors' offices, Golden Corral—as though I were a coat rack. I wish for that now, to be unobtrusive, part of the background. My khakis and gray turtleneck match the love seat. I could be camouflaged in the weave of the cushions. I cross my legs at the knee, my arms over my chest. I look down between the upholstery fibers, concentrate on a patch of foam where the threads have loosened. I squeeze into myself as though I might shrink small enough to slip through that hole and disappear.

"I'm so afraid she's gonna die," he says.

*

"Did I ever tell you why I got so sick?"

On the way to Las Cruces, before the hospital, before El Psychiatrist, the sun sat two fingers above the Organ Mountains. It was too warm for December, and yet my Grandpa kept the minivan heater at 75 degrees. I wanted to crack a window, but I didn't want to startle him. I wanted him to talk to me, to know that he could.

"I got separated from my unit," he said, not really looking at me.

For most of my life, he'd tell me stories about Dolores, the Texas ranch where he grew up, about coming to New Mexico for the Civilian Conservation Corps, and meeting my grandma outside a movie theater. He said she had the most beautiful legs. As I got older and did well in school, he'd say I must have gotten my brains from Grandma since she finished eighth grade, and he only got as far as elementary school. Once I left Deming for college and life beyond our one high school, one stoplight town, he'd ask on my visits home if I had a boyfriend and if I was working. When I moved back to my parents' house from El Paso right after Halloween, he seemed not to believe I was employed—how could I be here with him if I had a job? He, who grew up in the Depression and raised his children to get jobs with a pension, didn't understand consulting, how I'd pieced together an eclectic practice serving nonprofit organizations around the country.

This morning was different. He hadn't asked me about myself. He'd been quiet most of the drive. I imagined him replaying images from the weekend—Grandma coughing, her breath gurgling, the ambulance, the hospital, again. This setback had rattled something in him. What else would make him talk to me—to anyone—about the war? He talked, not exactly to me. It wasn't me that seemed to matter, but the telling.

"I'm alone in a field with trees all around the edges," he said, looking straight ahead as though the highway, and not me, spirited him to Grandma's sickbed. "I see something move in the corner of my eye. It's a Kraut. German. That's what we called them. I pull up my rifle."

*

El Psychiatrist's office feels windowless, even though slats of afternoon light filter through the closed copper blinds next to his desk. The window faces a parking lot. Shadows pass. People whose grandmothers aren't dying, who haven't moved back home because they can't handle sharing a town with Bad Boyfriend who never really loved them anyway, people who aren't listening to their grandpa tell his psychiatrist, "Dead people talk to me."

There's a black metal file cabinet with chrome handles in the corner opposite the loveseat. More file cabinets line the wall behind El Psychiatrist, folders and folders locked away, people's stories, their fears, their prognoses and disorders. Two wooden doctor figurines stand on one of the cabinets. Each wears a white lab coat and a stethoscope. They smile. She holds a clipboard. He writes a prescription. El Psychiatrist doesn't smile. He hardly looks up from the folder on his desk where he writes and writes, as though taking dictation.

"¿Quién, Señor Moran?"

I like that El Psychiatrist addresses my grandpa with respect, how calling him Señor restores some dignity he must lose by having a witness in his therapy sessions. It's always been this way. My grandpa has never been in a doctor's office alone. It's always been Grandma with him, asking questions, giving orders, filling out forms, keeping track. Maybe he's the lucky one. Maybe each of us needs someone to bear witness.

Grandpa talks without looking at me. I want to stare at him, study him. I want to ask who among the dead talks to him and what they say. The men he killed in the war, some part of Grandma that's already crossed over? A month from now, my grandma will be gone, and my mom will be the one on this couch. The psychiatrist will tell her that every day is an anniversary for Señor Moran. One trauma, un golpe, bleeds into the next and the next so he can't separate my grandma's death from the war from the psych ward from anything that's ever been hard. My whole life I've had the sense that he's never really *here*, that over breakfast he's tethering a donkey to a post in Dolores; he's running across a field, mortars lighting the night sky; he's separated from his unit; he's four years old and there's a new baby and his mother is dead. He's perpetually rain-soaked, swollen, held together with the stuff of earth, and over time, in drought, the memories turn to fine dust, become the air we breathe.

I don't know what to do with myself, what I am supposed to do, so I study the posters on the white brick wall behind El Psychiatrist in his dark brown suit and tie. Mini El Psychiatrists look out from an oval at the top of each poster. In the pictures, he wears a lab coat like the figurines.

Are you depressed? Do you suffer from more than one of the following?

I say I'm back home because my grandma is sick, but really, it's my own sickness that has brought me back. I need to be someplace that isn't El Paso, where Bad Boyfriend has his house and his university job, his books, his dog, and our writer friends. I have an empty apartment, a Harvard degree, a dying grandmother, and nothing to lift me out of the pit in which I find myself. I should be okay, but I'm not, and I don't know how to make myself better.

Difficulty sleeping or excessive exhaustion and sleeping too much.

I sleep ten, eleven hours a night.

I dream I drink a cup of dust. I scoop the bottom with a spoon, hold the cup in both hands and tilt my head back so I don't waste it.

*

"My rifle's stuck. I can't shoot," Grandpa said, crouching in the passenger seat.

The sun was three fingers above the Organs. I held my breath while Grandpa spoke, afraid he might stop talking, that I might never know this part of him.

"I'm down low," he said. "He's getting closer. Pero nada."

"His gun sticks too."

"Now he's running. Fast. With his…what do you call it? The blade?"

*

"¿Qué pasó?" El Psychiatrist asks.

My grandpa doesn't answer.

I rub my eyes. I glance from the poster to Grandpa to the psychiatrist. He's looking at me. His eyes are huge and blue, his face long and bony like a mad scholar or a wizard. His head is so smooth, almost shiny, but not from sweat, more like the sheen on Grandpa's shoes after my mom polishes them, which she's done once a week since Grandma had her lung removed.

"Es que…" even in English I don't know how to finish the sentence. My grandma has cancer, which is the same in English and Spanish. But she was home. She was fine.

"She doesn't really speak Spanish," Grandpa says, sparing me the embarrassment of my pocho accent.

"You can speak English," El Psychiatrist says.

"Gracias," I say, as surprised by his English as I was when he summoned me from the waiting room with "usted también."

"She gave us a scare," I say. I don't want to talk. Talking means I am here, and I shouldn't be. I don't want to be the adult in the room, the one

East / Tlahuitzlampa | 13

tracking prescriptions and appointments.

"What do you mean, a scare?" he asks, his shoulders as stiff and square as his photo on the Zoloft ad above the file cabinet. Zoloft. A Greek god. A superhero.

"She was strong when we brought her home right before Thanksgiving. The surgery went really well. She sat up in bed. She asked for coffee and her dentures. But then Saturday she couldn't breathe, and the hospital in Deming doesn't have doctors she needs, so they transferred her here to Las Cruces yesterday." I speak in past tense, as though we have come through something, as though it's over and she's home. "And now she's in critical care with pneumonia. But it's just pneumonia."

I don't yet know that her pneumonia will become Acute Respiratory Distress Syndrome, that she'll spend the rest of her life in critical care, that the rest of her life is less than a month. My grandpa is overreacting, I want to say. He worries too much. He's a nervous person. But I don't know what I am supposed to say, what I'm allowed to say. I don't know what this doctor knows or how far back into Grandpa's history I am supposed to travel. Does my grandpa reveal something new of himself with each visit? Or does he tell the same story, wrapping himself in memory until he is so tangled that only the doctor and my grandma can set him free?

El Psychiatrist turns back to my grandpa and says in his Italian-aria Spanish, "Lots of people get pneumonia. Hay una epidemia ahora."

*

When I was in preschool, Grandpa Tino hardly ever drove. When he did, it was to Saint Anne's for Saturday evening mass or to our house to drop off leftover calabacitas or beans "because Grandma says your mama's working and doesn't cook now that she has the microwave." On these occasions my grandma sat on the passenger side, conducting with one hand where he should turn, when to slow down or speed up. With the other hand, she dangled a cigarette out the window of their tan Buick Skylark, leaving a trail of smoke that would eventually lead them back home.

My grandma would pick me up from preschool while my parents were at work. Sometimes Grandpa waited for me at their house with a glass of whole milk and a plate of Oreos from the commissary on a TV tray in the living room. He'd sit on his recliner, and I'd sit on the couch, and together we'd watch a baseball game, a Western, or Lawrence Welk. Sometimes the house was silent and Grandpa was nowhere to be seen. Grandma would head straight to the back bedroom. "There's cookies in the cabinet, Michelley," she'd say. "And drink milk. No Coke." And I knew by the way she passed in and out of his room, like a note slipped through the door, that he was sick and I should not go to him or ask what was wrong. He was like a secret we hid, even from ourselves.

I'd look in their cabinets, opening and closing the metal doors with their magnet closures quietly so Grandma wouldn't catch me snooping. Black olives, sardines in oil, Quaker Oats, Snow Cap lard, Fig Newtons for Grandpa, Windmill Cookies for my mom, Oreos for me. I stood on the bottom shelf to reach the cabinet above the sink where she kept Grandpa's medicines. Rising from the contact paper vines, a stand of brown plastic bottles.

*

"Eso. A bayonet," Grandpa said, turning to look at me.

I turned my face toward his, enough so he knew I was with him, enough to see his chin quiver, before turning back to my hands on the steering wheel, the interstate, the semi-truck approaching in the rearview mirror.

"I think, Oh, Tino, you better hurry. You better get up.

"I put the blade.

"My legs feel heavy heavy, but I jump up. He still running, so I run. I lift the blade así." He raised his arms into striking position, an imaginary weapon in his hands. He trembled. The semi passed us. A stunted yucca on the roadside stood like a descanso.

*

If Grandpa was with Grandma when she picked me up from preschool, I knew that instead of going to their house, we were heading an hour away to Las Cruces and would probably have dinner there after his appointment.

Grandpa's first psychiatrist was Dr. Schmidt. He kept a basket of toys

East / Tlahuitzlampa | 15

for me under his desk where I'd sit linking and unlinking the cars of a wooden train set, rolling their black wheels past my grandparents' feet on one side and the doctor's, in his shiny brown shoes with leather tassels, on the other. Grandpa sat on his hands and bobbed his knees up and down. Grandma tapped the pads of her fingers on his thigh. Dr. Schmidt talked in a quiet voice like you do at church or a funeral.

"How are you sleeping, Mr. Moran?"

"He moves around too much," my grandma said.

"Nightmares?"

My grandpa nodded.

Visiting Dr. Schmidt was like visiting my grandparents' other friends, except my grandma would talk with her white voice and smile the same way she did when her dentures were out, not showing her teeth. He never checked my grandpa's heartbeat. He didn't even have a stethoscope. His office was like the boring room at the Deming library where old people read newspapers at rectangular tables and a special librarian stepped on a stool to pull the heaviest books down from the tallest shelves.

I didn't know what kind of sick my grandpa was, how driving an hour each way to talk to a nice white man would make him better or well, what better or well might look like for him, for us.

*

"Aim for the heart. That's what they taught us," he said, looking out the passenger window.

Alongside us ran the old highway and its tributaries of farm and county roads where my grandpa taught me to drive the summer between freshman and sophomore year. He showed me how to change a tire, how to maneuver across an arroyo in a summer storm. He showed me ghost towns, adobe homesteads built of mud, grass, shit, the stuff of earth, how they endured generations and crumbled slowly over time, only to return as dust, silt, or in the mud, grass, and shit of new adobes. He trusted me behind the wheel of his car, accelerating up to highway speeds, reversing out of his carport, taking the blind hill out of Spring Canyon. He never once raised his voice or reached for the wheel.

"It's different, mi'ja. Killing someone like that. With your hands. You can feel them die."

"I'm sorry, Grandpa," I said, taking a hand from the steering wheel and putting it on his. "I'm really sorry you had to do that. It wasn't your fault." He didn't flinch, didn't pull away. I wanted to stay with him like this, protected, the sun forever four fingers above the Organ Mountains, Grandma alive, my hand on Grandpa's, strong and still.

*

Was Dr. Schmidt the first to prescribe Prozac? Haloperidol? It was an antipsychotic, marketed under the brand name Haldol.

Early in the new year, after she dies and before the out-of-town cousins go home, we'll clear out and organize Grandma's files—credit card statements, newspaper clippings, photographs, greeting cards, casino earnings, VA letters stuffed in shoeboxes and bulk-size Quaker Oats boxes she kept in the utility room on wire-rack shelving above the extra freezer. I'll stack receipts for VA medication shipments on the area rug next to the big-screen television. Paxil and Xanax, older slips for Prozac and haloperidol.

Pills in the crystal ashtray, too nice for cigarettes. Pastels, reds, tiny letters in white or black, clear capsules filled with candy beads.

*

Children teeter-totter in a picture frame on the shelf behind El Psychiatrist's desk.

"If I could trade my life for hers, I would," Grandpa says while the doctor depresses a two-hole punch onto the papers in his hand, then straightens and lowers them onto the open brackets of a manila folder.

From above his desk, mini El Psychiatrists check for signs of depression: *Poor self-image. Feelings that you look old or unattractive.*

Sometimes I am—ugly. And I guess sometimes I'm beautiful. I don't really pay attention.

That's not true.

I examine my face every night and morning, squeezing blackheads between my pinkies and scraping away the hair-like sacs clogging my pores. I guess I'm thin, but not like a model. I have my Grandma China's long legs, a soft belly, and gentle curves. Bad Boyfriend once said I have

East / Tlahuitzlampa | 17

an Audrey Hepburn neck. He was drunk. But I think he meant it.

*

I think the tremors started when I was in kindergarten. He'd talk about his childhood, about basic training, the ship that took him to France. I stayed away from him then. Instead of sitting on the couch while he rocked on the recliner, I'd sit in the kitchen with my mom and grandma.

"He can't remember what he had for breakfast," my grandma said.

At home, my mom told my dad, "They think he has Alzheimer's."

He couldn't stop trembling. They told my grandma he had Parkinson's.

We didn't know the side effects of Haldol—muscle spasms, stiffness, shaking or tremors, restlessness, mask-like facial expression, drooling. This was my grandpa those years I was in preschool, kindergarten, first and second grade. I wondered: Why does he move like that? What's wrong with him? We didn't know that years of Haldol would cause tardive dyskinesia, that the chances of getting TD go up the longer one takes an antipsychotic, that for some, for my grandpa, TD meant the stiff, jerky movements were permanent.

We didn't know that the drugs he was given to treat TD might cause depression.

He broke. No one in the family said it, but what else could we call Grandpa sitting on his living room recliner, rocking back and forth, not talking, staring at a blank television screen?

Grandpa squatting and turning the television dial, a machine gun rat-a-tatting past Bonanza–Braves–Ricky Ricardo–Big Bird. He lands on a laugh track. I think he'll go back to his chair. But he turns the knob again, Colonel Klink–Jeannie–Get Smart–SWAT. He turns the knob again. And again. He does this all afternoon.

Grandpa marching along the fence like he's on patrol, from one end of the front yard to the other and back.

Grandpa running after high school kids in a green Mustang. "Slow down!" he yells, scooping a fistful of dirt and hurling it toward the street.

Grandpa locking himself in the bathroom and threatening to swallow all of his pills. I wasn't there for that part. No one told me the story. Over the years it broke apart and scattered. I'm trying to sweep up the pieces, to reshape them into a story that heals us.

*

I don't know if my grandpa came out on his own or if my mom kicked the door in, if she found him passed out or standing in the tub fully clothed. I don't know if an ambulance was called or his stomach pumped, if he really took the pills or turned the prescription bottles over the toilet and flushed.

I only know that after that day, he got worse before he got better. He ended up in the VA psych ward in Albuquerque. I don't know how she did it, how she made them listen, but my grandma made the doctors take him off every medication. She made them start again with nothing, just my grandpa and his memories.

*

Irritability and frustration. Feelings of anger and resentment.
I wish I were pissed off. I miss October, miss the surge of leaving Bad Boyfriend alone in his house with the broken bedroom window and the panting swamp cooler, his yard-sale furniture covered in black dog hair. I miss November, the first day back in my parents' house, one day before my grandma's diagnosis, unloading my books, lighting a candle, hoping by the time it was out, I'd be over Bad Boyfriend, I'd be well. It's almost Christmas, and I still can't breathe. I feel I am underwater, but my lips crack and I'm always thirsty.

Bad Boyfriend is gone; my sadness is not. A year from now, when I am learning Spanish in Mexico, I will tell a friend, "Yo estaba deprimida." He will say, "No, you mean you were sad. Depressed is super sad, more sad than you could ever be."

I will have my own medication then, five milligrams of Lexapro. I will learn the words to tell my own story—recuerdos, trauma, sobreviviente, abuso sexual.

If I were my grandpa I would ask me to leave the room. But he doesn't. Or maybe he can't. Illness exposes, breaks us, and in the breaking we give ourselves to others whether we want to or not. So I sit. And wait. And wonder about the German my grandpa killed with his hands, the one he told me about this morning in the car. Will my grandpa ever be at peace?

"Aumentamos el medicamento."

East / Tlahuitzlampa | 19

El Psychiatrist's eyes are on me again. I nod as he rips a page off his prescription pad.

Grandpa scoots to the edge of his chair and stands, motioning to me for his coat and hat.

"With the Paxil it's very important he take it every day. If he skips a dose, he'll definitely feel it." I scribble "Paxil—More" on the legal pad and then stand, my hands full—Grandpa's fedora and jacket, my backpack, the legal pad, my keys. I don't know anything—milligrams, what time to give him which drugs, which doctors to call, how to order his medications or special shoes from the VA. We don't know anything.

"When do you want to see him again?" I ask.

"I'll be back from vacation in five weeks," he says, extending his arm to hand me Grandpa's prescription.

"He's going to Argentina, mi'ja."

"That's nice," I say, nodding and smiling without showing my teeth. My hands are full, so I motion toward the loveseat with my chin.

"He's from there."

"Let me get an appointment card for you," El Psychiatrist says, setting the prescription on an armrest. "Please excuse me." He steps out of the room.

"Are you hungry, Grandpa?" I ask.

He shakes his head.

I unload my arms onto the cushion with the hole. I hand him his hat, which I know he will hold until we are outside because it's rude to wear a hat in a building.

His face twists. His eyes search for a spot to focus. He looks up then down at the floor like he does when we say grace for meals, as though pulling God's blessing down to earth. He sways. His face jerks. He seems to always be saying *yes*, not yeah, or uh-huh, but a thoughtful, methodic *yes...yes.*

Grandma China will be dead in less than a month. Grandpa Tino will live five long and lonely years without her, and the night he dies, the sadness will lift from their house.

"You understand the things I said, mi'jita?"

I nod. "Yeah, Grandpa. I understand Spanish."

I should have said no. I shouldn't know these things about him. Or if I do, I should offer him something in return—a doctor who touches his hands, a friend who knew him before the war, before the breakdowns, someone who knew him when he was whole, who saw him break apart and loved him anyway, someone to seal the cracks in him with spit and masa, who could sew the fissures with her own hair, with fibers from her own muscles. Isn't that what we all want? Someone who can love through the breaking.

"Oh," he says, looking toward the door, "I hope you're not disappointed in me."

"I could never be disappointed in you," I say. And because he's still not looking at me or maybe he didn't hear, or what I've given doesn't feel like enough, I add, "You should hear what I tell my therapist," and I kind of laugh. What I tell my therapist, and will tell and retell, about my own memories, the battles little girls fight—to keep older boys from touching us. Neighbor. Brother. All I've done to be well—journaling, limpias, therapy, meds. How it can all fall apart when a boyfriend is bad, when a grandmother is dying. There are some things I don't ever want my grandpa to know.

I hold Grandpa's windbreaker open for him. He steps into it like an out-of-shape boxer. I take his hand to lead him out of the doctor's office. He trembles. He shakes.

We are the color of adobe, weathered earth, fired clay.

That week between hospital stays, Grandpa declares his intentions to Grandma

Vieja, we don't have to move in with the kids. I'll take care of you. Siempre te voy a cuidar.

Grandma replies

Tino, you don't know nothing.

Grandpa Dreams
after

    We were taking a trip in that old pickup I used to have. China was sitting next to me. The kids were little and they rode in the truck bed. We drove through a meadow in Tejas, and the clouds were low-low like they are today. The truck broke down 'cause they used Japanese parts. I told them don't use Japanese parts.

    I couldn't find your mama or your uncle. I turn to your Grandma y le digo, *Where's Cookie and Perry?* but she doesn't answer. She wore a long dress like they did in the pioneer days and long-sleeves with a belt made of cloth y un moño aquí to the side. And a hat like the women used to protect them from the sun.

    I ask her again, *Where's Cookie y Perry?* But she don't answer me. It's your grandma, but I can't see her face.

    I can't see her face, mi'ja.

    I'm going to write that dream. It has to be in Spanish. The spelling will be wrong.

Grandpa Vows
after

I won't take off my wedding ring as long as I'm alive.

Grandpa Vows
after

I promise not to get married again.

What Grandpa says when a friend invites him to shoot pool as a way to get him out of the house
after

Me with a stick. I probably couldn't even hit the mountain.

Sweatpants
winter—after

Grandpa wears a sweatshirt the color of duct tape. It's tucked into the heather-blue sweatpants he wore yesterday and the day before. They ride high, revealing a band of skin above slouched white tube socks and black dress shoes with thick soles. I've convinced him that the only way I can drop the "thank you for your kindness during this difficult time" ad at the *Deming Headlight* office is if he picks me up and drives. Because he has left his house, he wears a hat, plaid tweed with a green feather, something between a fedora and Irish wool. His tan windbreaker seems too thin for the ashy clouds gathering above the Florida Mountains, their tops visible from my parents' cul de sac where he parks his little white pickup truck. Like always, he opens the door for me and walks around the back to the driver side door.

January is the ugliest month in Deming. Everything burnt charcoal, ash. Even my black hair is dull here, the ends coarse like the grass in my parents' front yard. Minutes before Grandpa picked me up, I changed into the same faded jeans, gray turtleneck, and black fleece I wear on those rare occasions when I go out in public. My skirts and tights, heels, boots, and blouses with buttons and collars hang unused in the closet. Since I got here almost three months ago I've ironed only once, for my grandma's funeral. These errands never take enough time, and too soon Grandpa will be back in his house alone, and I will be back in my parents' house, wearing my younger brother's cross-country joggers with their soft cotton lining and dried mud flaking off the hems.

We pass a trailer park where I used to sell Girl Scout cookies, walking up and down gravel streets named for dead white writers most of us had never read—Tennyson, Kipling, Emerson. I used to think these were the rich people, the old white ladies from somewhere else who came here for the altitude and mild weather. Snow birds with their paved roads, their neat yards of raked gravel, their porches carpeted in squares of fake grass held in place by container gardens of rosemary, mint, and cactus, the same romero, hierba buena y nopal growing wild in the undeveloped lots we all referred to as the mesquites. As in, *Let's walk the shortcut to Grandma's through the mesquites.* Or, *Don't go too far into the mesquites. You never know who could be out there.* The snow bird ladies always had pristine welcome mats, and their groomed Chihuahuas, poodles, and weenie dogs always barked before I tapped on the screen door.

Grandpa's Old Spice, heavier today than usual, fills the air between us in the truck. I crack my window and breathe in the clean cold, its sharpness the only part of winter in Deming I like, the one thing fierce and alive in the midst of so much death.

We pass the t-ball fields and more trailers on Calle Juan and Calle Jaime, newer streets that look more like alleyways with lopsided mobile homes squeezed between cinderblock stilts and old tires holding down tarpaper roofs. A broken washing machine sits in a dirt yard. A boy and girl play in the bed of an abandoned truck.

Bell School, where my mom has been a teacher for more than twenty years, is a block building with chain basketball nets on the outdoor court and skinny maples lining the perimeter of the dirt playground. My dad was in the first class to attend this school, when the district moved all the brown kids from a rundown building with basement classrooms to a brand new school with shiny floors and white walls. Like Mexico City, it was built on sand and marsh. It sank into the ground and had to be rebuilt.

We pass Chicano Park, a triangle of dry grass with two concrete picnic tables and a metal slide too hot to touch in summer months.

"You think those clouds over the Floridas will give us some snow or rain?" I ask.

Since the New Year, they only spit at us, dusting our windows and cars, but never soaking the ground.

"I don't know, mi'ja. I don't know anything since Grandma's gone."

"Yeah," I say, taking a deep breath. "I know."

He's right. We don't know anything—how to make her red chile or that caldo de todo she'd prepare on a day like today with whole Brussels sprouts and chunks of stew meat, how to mix a Jack and Coke, how to grieve together. Since she died, it's each of us in our own misery—Mom crying in the shower, me awake at night, wanting sleep, wanting to dream her, Grandpa in a dark house surrounded by objects she touched, clothes she wore, stuff she bought, not allowing us to move anything.

We cut across gem streets, Diamond and Ruby, the St. Ann's steeple rising above block houses on uneven ground. I've been holding the folder with our thank you ad and a ten-dollar bill paper-clipped to it. Grandpa pulls into the *Deming Headlight* parking lot, which never seems to have more than two cars. Once outside the truck, he stands up straight and tucks his hands inside the waistband of his sweatpants. With his hands tucked into his pants, he grabs the bottom of his sweatshirt and stretches it down until his arms are buried elbow deep and his clavicle is exposed above his crewneck. As he withdraws his hands from his pants, careful not to dislodge the sweatshirt, he grabs the waistline of his sweats and pulls up, the way he might pull a blanket to his chest to sleep. I try not to stare at him, to give him this moment to right himself and feel comfortable in his clothes, if not his skin.

The Headlight office still has its wood-paneled walls and drop ceiling. I half-expect to see the reporter turned editor in the same oversized T-shirt and biker shorts he wore all through my junior high and high school years when he'd cover little league, track meets, bowling tournaments, honor society inductions, parades, homecoming and prom, and the state student council convention I coordinated my senior year. He'd arrive with his reporter's notebook in hand, a camera strapped around his neck and resting on his belly.

The woman at the front desk tells me the ad will run in two days as she hands back my change.

"I want to stop at the Snappy Mart," Grandpa says as we get back in the truck. "The Power Ball is thirty-eight million."

Once a week, or more often when the jackpot is high, he buys one ticket for him, one for my mom, one for Grandma—which is really for him—and now that I am back, one for me.

"Sounds good, Grandpa."

At the Snappy Mart, he fills the truck with gas and then drives us across the parking lot to a space a few steps from the door. Over the last several years, my grandma racked up more than forty thousand dollars in credit card debt. Television with surround sound, treadmill, My parents now manage Grandpa's bank accounts. With his veteran's pension and social security, the house paid off, and the credit cards destroyed, my dad says they can knock out the debt in about eighteen months. Sooner, if one of us wins the PowerBall.

Tickets in hand, Grandpa gives me the truck keys and says, "You drive, mi'ja. Go through downtown, so you can see the new things."

The old movie theater is now Nena's Fashions. I can't imagine what it's like inside or how Nena stays in business. The building next door was another clothing store where they sold factory second Levis. Our band director made a deal with the owners for a special rate on the white jeans we'd wear for casual gigs and jazz band. When it went out of business, there was a push by high school students and teachers to turn the building into a youth center. The City invested in a chain link fence to enclose a segment of the parking lot and installed basketball goals at opposite ends, one drilled right into the building, the other a portable unit wheeled in at night. They claimed further improvements weren't in the budget. That was the same year they expanded the golf course from nine to eighteen holes.

"See the turn arrow, mi'ja?" Grandpa asks at the stoplight.

"Yeah, pretty fancy, Grandpa." When I was growing up, Deming had three stoplights and one flashing four way stop on the south edge of town to slow down ranchers and cotton trucks coming in from the fields.

The hairdresser, office supply, and department store once lining Gold Street are gone, replaced by an evangelical church and a Christian bookstore. The temperature on the electronic bank marquee reads forty-nine degrees.

SouthSide Market went under not long after WalMart opened for business. Planned Parenthood sat behind it, the front entrance facing the busiest street in town, the back facing Holy Family Catholic Church. When I was in high school, Deming had the highest teen pregnancy rate in New Mexico, which had the highest teen pregnancy rate in the country.

We pull into the mall parking lot. The mall is built of corrugated metal and has four storefronts, two of which are empty. Farmers Market will close by the end of the year, leaving only Family Dollar.

"Go to the handicapped, mi'ja," Grandpa says, opening the glove compartment and pulling out his permit. He hangs it from the rearview mirror. I imagine a permit for our handicap—stick figure slouched in a corner, face half in shadow. Grandpa is a World War Two veteran with Post-Traumatic Stress Disorder, anxiety, and depression. I am a survivor of a car accident, a Bad Boyfriend, and childhood sexual abuse, which seems to seep into everything, even the stuff I'm good at, which is a lot, and never enough. And I am tired of talking about it, or maybe tired of who I'm talking to—therapist, other survivors, my journal, writers who write about sexual abuse. I'm tired of who I don't talk to, what I keep from my family, and yet, the thought of bringing them into this story makes me even more tired. How to tend to them and care for myself, how to keep from conversations about what happened, when and how, and why I didn't tell, how to control the narrative. And so I keep this story to myself—until the time comes when I can't anymore, when the silence no longer holds.

The stark blue shards of the Floridas cut into the clouds, spreading gray above and around us. Under this sky, the mountains seem taller, fertile, a place where streams could smooth and polish stones. But I know those mountains. The plants—yucca, ocotillo, prickly pear—hurt to touch, protecting themselves to survive drought, rattlesnakes, cattle, drunks, flash floods. Each of us deserves a set of thorns when the threat is great, or perhaps, like the locust tree, a spine that grows into a seedpod only when the branches are strong enough to survive, maybe thrive.

*

"Eight for three dollars. Better than the K-Mart, no?" my grandpa asks, gesturing toward the double A batteries labeled with a number three, big and red, like all the numbers at this store. "For the remote control in the bedroom."

"Looks like a good deal, Grandpa," I say, nodding and patting his shoulder.

He gets two packs from the rack and walks toward the checkout stand.

"You don't need to go nowhere else, mi'ja?"

"No, Grandpa," I say. "But you should come for dinner. Mom's making enchiladas."

"Oh…" he says, eyeing the candy display in the checkout line.

"You're not hungry?"

"I have chicken."

"From where?"

"The Wal-Mart."

"Grandpa, that food isn't made with love. Eat with us. Please. We want you to."

"We'll see," he says, which really means no or I don't want to or I'd rather go home and sleep.

"You don't want a candy?" he asks. "I'll get you a candy."

"No thanks, Grandpa," I say.

I should have said yes. I should have let my grandpa buy me a candy bar. I want to take it back, say, *Yes, Grandpa, I'd love a candy. Candy would make me happy.* But he's put the batteries on the counter, and a couple is now behind us in line, their bodies between Grandpa and the Snickers, PayDay, and peanut butter cups.

The man in front of us tilts a box of Sun laundry soap toward the checker so she can scan the price. He shakes his head when the checker reaches for a plastic bag. The man looks older than my grandpa, less cared for, made of dust.

The checker in her red smock hands him his change, and he leaves. He crosses the parking lot, then the street on foot, then vanishes into the line of cinderblock houses and chain link fences behind the Beverage Corner, where a guy I dated briefly in high school worked after his family got busted in an international drug smuggling operation, the largest bust in state history. They owned a beauty salon, a house south of town on two acres of land enclosed by a six-foot concrete wall, and a champion racehorse they housed in an air-conditioned horse stall north of town.

Grandpa hands the batteries to the checker and steps back from the register. He slides his hands down his pants, fists bulging against blue fleece as he grasps the bottom of the sweatshirt and pulls. I imagine the hem falling to his knees like the nightshirts Grandma wore between hospital stays. He slides his forearms out from the sweatpants and pulls the waistband up again. There's a thumbnail-sized rip at the crotch of his sweatpants.

My grandma would be embarrassed. She always had him looking so nice. My mom spends part of her weekends ironing trousers and collared shirts for him, but they hang untouched in his closet, across from my grandma's clothes. I miss his sweaters, his Dockers. I miss the pristine mechanic coveralls he wore long after he closed his shop. He ties the white drawstring at mid-torso. It sticks straight out like a loop I might tug to lead him through the store or back to the truck or maybe into a life without my grandma, a life where he is useful, productive, like a man.

Pesado
winter—after

High on my grandpa's cheekbone, under his left eye, blood congeals on what looks like a shaving cut, except that it's on a hairless part of his face.

"What happened?" I ask, as he holds onto my arm and steps out of the van.

"Oh," he says, looking past me toward the toll of bells from St. Ann's church across the street. "Dreams, I guess."

"We'll have to get you some mittens—like those sleepers they have for babies."

He doesn't laugh at my joke, doesn't even smile. He straightens his fedora and walks past me toward the entrance to St. Ann's.

My grandma would have made him wipe the blood from his face. *You can't go out like that, Tino.*

We reach the wooden door of the church together. I hold it open for him, and he pats my head as he passes into the entryway. He dips his fingers into the holy water font and crosses his forehead and murmurs to himself, to his dead wife, to St. Ann and La Virgen, maybe even to me, "Es muy duro, mi'ja. Pesa mucho."

Grandpa Dreams
after

This time she talked to me. 'stamos en El Doctor's office. She's wearing a short dress like when she was young. You could see her legs. She was sitting and she had people all around her. Needles y blood pressure y todo. When I walk in she looks up and says to me, *They're gonna pump you full of pills.*

Grandpa Vows
after

I promise not to kill myself. I
won't. I won't
kill myself. I
promise.

Grandpa Dreams
after

To tell you the truth, I think she just wants me to leave her alone.

West / Cihuatlampa

puesta de sol
rumbo de las mujeres
donde todo lo innecesario se entrega

positive

indicating the presence of a disease, condition, or organism, as a diagnostic test

the spot on her lung

a plus sign

a cross

Caliche

winter—before, hours before, during

She passed on January 3, 2004 on a bed of white sheets in a hospital in Las Cruces, an hour from Deming, where my grandpa first met her when he was a Texas boy with the Civilian Conservation Corps and she was a light-skinned, long-legged fourteen-year-old who learned to smoke by studying him. She died of lung cancer, pneumonia, and Acute Respiratory Distress Syndrome. She died as my grandfather, my mom and dad, uncles and aunts and great uncles and brothers and cousins and nieces and nephews and I blessed her forehead with crosses and kisses, caressed her feet and hands, and sang Las Mañanitas, as though it were a day of birth.

Alone and silent, she passed for white. The gabachos confided in her, couples trading spouses at the Country Club where she waited tables when my mom was a girl, snowbirds from Minnesota and Nebraska who packed Deming's RV parks during our mild winters and stood next to her in line at the Safeway. When a Mexican mother with too many children cut in front of her, a white woman stage-whispered to my grandma, "We don't do that where I'm from." Stepping around the lady toward the front of the line, my grandma said, "Then you should go back there."

She passed on before she should have, not two months after her bad lung was removed, not an hour after the machines were disconnected.

She passed before I could marry, before I could give love and get it back, before I could finish graduate school, or tell our stories. She passed when I still needed her. We all did. We still do.

*

"How's your grandmother?" Stephanie asks as I take the seat next to her in the reading room turned lecture hall at Vermont College. We sit along a wall of books as built in as the shelves holding them. We are a few days into the winter residency of our graduate program in creative writing. It's New Year's Day, 2004, and I've slept through dining hall breakfast hours.

My stomach growls.

Our professor approaches the lectern at the front of the room. A beauty queen in her twenties, now in her fifties, she is pretty and polished with olive skin, streaks of silver in her bobbed haircut, blue-green eyes, and a style that could glide from lecture hall to ski resort.

"The respirator has through the weekend to work," I whisper, taking off my gloves and jacket. "Then we'll decide…" I can't feel my body for the cold, for my JC Penney long johns, the jeans I wore last night, the black turtleneck I wear every time I leave the dorm, a bulky wool sweater, fleece pullover, wool socks, hiking boots, and REI sale bin hat that doesn't completely cover my ears. I hate wearing so much, the constant dressing and undressing from outdoor to indoor and back again.

It's only Thursday, less than halfway through the residency. My essay collection on death and ghosts will be critiqued in two days. I wrote about my dad's side of the family, the one I thought held all the stories. I wrote about my Grandma Rosie, my dad's mom, the nice grandma who died when I was a freshman at Harvard studying for first semester finals. Her real name was Rosaura. She and my Grandpa Paul, whose real name was Pantaleón, gave their children names they thought sounded American: Oliver, Ralph, Elbert. My mom and I picked her up every Sunday for mass; she wore nude knee-high stockings and a black mantilla to cover her hair. I wrote about two first cousins I never met, brothers. One died in a fire when he was a child. The other played with matches. He lived another thirty years, then hung himself in his front yard. I wrote about how the grief broke their parents' marriage, the copper mine where my uncle—and so many brown men—made their living, and the waste of a mountain left behind once all the value was extracted. I wrote about the women of Juárez, about a poet I once kissed who took his own life, about all the ways we don't heal.

"I can leave right after the workshop and be home by Saturday night. That still gives me a day."

"Oh Michelle," she says. "We need to get you home."

I look at my lap, at her hand on mine, red from the cold. I close my eyes and take a deep breath. I know she's right. I know my grandma won't survive the weekend. But I am waiting for my workshop critique, for a change drastic enough to call me home, for someone in my family to tell me I am needed, that my grandma can't die without me next to

West / Cihuatlampa | 43

her. But we don't say things in my family, not the things we should say. And yet, truth comes without our calling. She is already dying, whether I am next to her or across the country. I know with her death my Grandpa Tino will slip from us behind the closed door of his memories, World War II, the psych ward, the dead, just as he did when I was a child and the words we knew for depression and trauma were *Grandpa's sick.*

Grief will twist itself around his body as soon as the out of town cousins and tíos load up their rental cars and drive back to Austin or Albuquerque or the El Paso airport, twist like the sheet around his feet and flannel pajama legs, holding him to the queen bed where he will sleep in sunlight and watch Gunsmoke reruns in the dark.

I blink my eyes. Stephanie squeezes my hand and then picks up her notebook and pen.

"Go ahead and impose yourself on the world," the professor says, beginning her lecture on Urgency in Memoir.

My phone vibrates through my backpack, against my foot. A call. A voicemail. I am out of minutes.

"We are indignant when pain visits us," my professor says. "We write from a place of why me, how could this happen, what did I do to deserve."

Another call. Two voicemails. More and more calls.

I scribble a note to Stephanie and pat her hand. Here in Vermont, we feel like the only women of color in the universe. I am the Latina. Stephanie and Karen are African American. There are two Asian fiction writers, a Black poet who grew up on Long Island, and Harrison, who looks white, but whose mom is a Chicana artist from New Mexico. Karen, Stephanie, and I have formed a protective bubble around one another, escaping down the hill during summer residency to Ben & Jerry's after a white woman in the program asked Karen if she might read a draft of her memoir about the Black housekeeper and nanny who raised her. Now in winter we traveled here together, meeting in New York, bolstering for the snow, the whiteness, the inevitable "What's your heritage? No, really, where are you *from* from?"

"I'll be right back," I mouth to her. She nods.

The door squeaks. From the lectern, my professor asks, "Who are you to be spared?"

*

The phone booth is the size of a coat closet with a folding chair, a tabletop bolted to the wall and a window facing the reading room door. I call for messages using the prepaid phone card my parents gave me for the trip.

"They're putting a tube in her throat," my brother says in one message.

"I can pick you up wherever, El Paso, Albuquerque, even if it's late. Let me know," he says in another.

"The specialist wants to incubate," my mom says. I think of third grade and the half-dozen duck eggs our class kept in a glass mother with one bare light bulb and straw for warmth. Each duckling died after cracking its shell, one revealing a beak, another, one closed eye.

It wasn't supposed to be this way. The oncologist told my grandma she was lucky. He said, "Most people don't have the option of living with one lung."

After the pneumonectomy, our job was to get her ready for chemo. I stayed on her couch the weekend after surgery so I could cook for her and make her morning coffee, but she woke earlier than I did. Always. She didn't need me so I went back to my parents' house, back to their spare bedroom, away from El Paso and Bad Boyfriend, and close to what, I didn't know.

I slipped back to El Paso on the Feast Day of Our Lady of Guadalupe for a friend's book release. She read her poetry under white Christmas lights in a crumbling mission on the edge of town, her audience sipping chocolate, Mexican blankets on our laps.

"Meet us at the hospital," my mom called to say as I drove back to Deming the next day. "Grandma has pneumonia." My cell lost signal as a border agent waved me through the checkpoint.

When I walked into her room, my grandma was sitting up in bed. She turned to me and said, "See what happens when you leave?"

*

"Please stay on the line and the next available representative will be with you shortly. American Airlines appreciates your patience."

My professor with her Oil of Olay complexion steps into a circle of admiring students in tailored coats and stylish winter boots and hats.

West / Cihuatlampa | 45

They beam out of my field of vision, back into the snow where they will cross the commons and sit together for lunch. Our chefs are students at the New England Culinary Institute. Depending on where they are in their studies, the meals they prepare are either first-semester rough drafts or close to homemade—if home is white and in Vermont.

I grind the hangnail on my ring finger until my teeth can't reach it. Then I start on the nail, at first biting, then chewing straight through and spitting granules to the floor.

"American Airlines, how may I help you?"

I don't know where to start, what to say.

"I'm trying to get home."

There are change fees for each leg of the trip, an increase in ticket price. Nothing out of Burlington will get me back to New Mexico tonight. Maybe Albany, if I can get a ride or rent a car. I could fly from there into Phoenix or Tucson. $800. Overnight. First class. Denver. Albuquerque. I scrawl on the back of my manuscript. Points on a map. Death and ghosts.

Please speak slowly. I want to say. *Please be nice to me.* I'm hunched over the bolted table, my head in my free hand.

"I don't know what to do," I say to the agent, a stranger.

The door opens. Stephanie. She puts one hand on my shoulder and with the other, transfers the receiver from my ear to hers.

"Hi, I'm a friend of Ms. Otero's," she says in a calm voice. "We're trying to get her as close to Las Cruces, New Mexico as possible. Yes, tonight. What are our options?"

She writes departure cities and times in neat rows on a crisp sheet of notebook paper. Her fingernails are trimmed and clean. I stare at her free ear, how it comes to a soft point at the top, and how this, combined with her dark eyes and high cheekbones give her the look of a fairy or an angel sent to get me home. "Thank you" and "yes, please" and "I appreciate it" into the phone. She hangs up and turns to me.

"You're flying out of Albany this afternoon. Karen and I are taking you. She's getting directions off of MapQuest. I'll talk to administration. Go to your room and pack. We'll meet you there," she says, handing me a strawberry yogurt, a plastic spoon, and an apple that must have been with her when she entered the booth but seemed to materialize only as she put them in my hands.

*

It shouldn't surprise any of us that my grandma would spend her final days short of breath. In every photograph over a forty-year period she holds a cigarette between her long, thin fingers. Virginia Slims for ladies and later filtered Kent III 100's. Here and now, intubated in critical care, it doesn't matter that hypnosis kept her clean for fifteen years, not even a craving. But she gained weight and her hands fidgeted. She sorted beans, played solitaire, picked at our pimples, dug out our splinters with a sewing needle and tweezers sterilized on a gas flame.

I was a little girl the first time she quit cold turkey. She threw out the carton on top of her fridge and cleaned the house from back to front with Pine Sol and bleach.

The yellow phone rang in our kitchen. My mom answered. She sucked air through her teeth and hung up.

"Put on your shoes. Grandma's sick."

We lived two minutes from Grandma's house. Like always, the tan Buick with the white top was parked in the dirt outside the block wall where my cousins and I had pressed our hands into wet cement and wrote our names with sticks in the block closest to the gate. My uncles built it with Grandpa last summer when he still came outside and people still visited.

Mom let us in with her key. The kitchen shade was closed even though it was the middle of the day. Mornings before Grandpa woke up, my grandma would sit at the table smoking, drinking black coffee, and watching farm trucks roll past the house carrying chile, onions, cotton, and Mexicanos to and from the gabacho fields, ranches, and chile plant south of town.

I didn't see Grandpa, but I knew he was in his bedroom, like always.

Grandma China lay on her stomach in bed. The old slip she wore as a nightgown was rolled to her shoulders. I'd never seen so much of her skin. Her back was almost white and scattered with freckles and moles like the brown spots on tortillas fresh off the comal. My other grandma, the nice one who never learned to drive and could hardly hear, made tortillas every day. But this grandma only made them for special occasions and only if we asked. They tasted smoky like her hugs.

My grandma was a tall woman with long legs and a big voice that reached every corner of the house when she was angry. She was always cooking or washing dishes, driving my grandpa to doctor appointments, scrubbing the kitchen floor on hands and knees, frying corn tortillas and dipping them in a vat of red chile on the stove. She was never sick. What was happening to her? Was she dying? Would her skin burn my fingers?

I wanted to touch her, but I stayed at her feet, out of the way, which my mom always said was the best way for me to help. Outside the sun was late morning high, but inside her bedroom felt cool like the corners of an adobe church. Light dripped through the backyard window onto the sheets bunched at my grandma's waist, her back, her rolled up nightgown, the wisps of brown hair sticking up on her head. I didn't speak.

My grandma gestured to a tub of butter or margarine on the night table next to her bed.

The table, matching dresser, and headboard took up so much space my mom had to turn sideways to fit between the bed and the wall. She scooped butter from the tub on the night table and rubbed it on Grandma's back and legs.

Why butter? I don't know. She spoke to my mother in Spanish, and my mother nodded her head, breathed in through her mouth, and exhaled *mmmms* and *oooohs*. Did butter break a fever? Did cigarettes dry her skin? I didn't speak Spanish. I would learn years later in college classes, a summer in Guatemala, and a Fulbright in Mexico. This morning, a little girl in my grandma's house, I didn't understand what she said or how my mom was helping. But just like at Mass when we'd sing *Maravilloso Es* and my eyes were closed and my heart felt the kind of warm my brothers and I would jockey for when we'd shove each other for the spot in front of Grandma's wall heater, I understood the butter, my mother's hands, the soft light, even my presence at Grandma's knees was important, healing, that this act repeated would make her well. And it did—for a time. It was only later I understood that cigarettes were more powerful than any of us. My grandma couldn't quit. Quitting made her sick and fat, nervous and grouchy. Within a month, the carton was back on top of her fridge, the Slims back between her fingers, and all her food tasted of ash.

*

I take bites of the apple between pulling turtlenecks and sweaters from wire hangers and folding them into the black suitcase my dad won in a raffle at last year's company Christmas party. The hard plastic lining inside the suitcase cracked at some point, scattering stucco-like chips through my socks and underwear. I find them pressed to my hip or ankle at day's end, the skin chafed red.

The fruit is winter, grainy, its skin waxy and thick. I toss the core through the window I opened after midnight when the air was so dry I could hardly swallow. I think of my grandmother's mouth without teeth, how her cheeks and lips soften and sink each night as her dentures soak in their blue plastic case. I picture her body the same way, as though her lungs held up her ribs and now that one is missing, she must be half-collapsed. The apple vanishes in the snow.

I zip my suitcase and sit on the floor to wait for Stephanie and Karen. I lean against the bed, its metal frame a cold bar across my shoulders. I stare at the empty closet, wooden rack, paint peeling, wire hangers bare and motionless.

The door to my room is open. The radiator knocks. I don't turn in my room keys. I don't shower. The shared bathrooms are down the hall. I brought body wash with exfoliating moisture beads but no washcloth or bath puff and can't scrub my knees, elbows, or feet with anything but my hands. I think of my mom, how dirt in our elbows embarrassed her when we were kids. I remember the last time she bathed me. Was I six? Seven? Steam rose from my arms as I lifted them out of the tub. The water, my mother's hands, the time she took, the way she shook her head when she scoured the back of my ankles with a washcloth made me feel loved and shamed at the same time. Now I set the bathwater to red. Nothing less washes me clean.

*

Karen, Stephanie, and I stop at a gas station on our way out of town. I fill a foam cup with coffee machine mocha. The clerk in his red smock stares at us. Or maybe everyone does. Karen's locs, Stephanie's pulled back hair, her tasteful handbag, new Volvo at pump number three. And me.

West / Cihuatlampa | 49

I don't know how I look, how anyone can see me under so many layers, my brown skin faded to gray under Vermont's low skies. I am a shadow, not fully formed in this time zone, this season, this place. Vermont is tall trees in the distance, white clapboard houses with A-shaped roofs, dirty snow in mounds by train tracks. A storm is coming, bringing more snow, wind and ice. I've never understood how this part of the country got to be the birthplace of our nation, the seat of learning, the standard by which we are to measure ourselves. If the founding fathers had exercised better judgment, they'd have kept moving west toward warmer temperatures and longer growing seasons. I don't believe we humans are meant to live in these places, covering ourselves from the cold, in constant need of shelter from a climate that fights so hard against us.

We drive for two hours before realizing we're going the wrong way, that Karen's MapQuest search excluded interstate highways and major roads. We don't know where we are or which road will get us to Albany, and so we keep driving through farms, boroughs, villes, each as gray as the last.

My mom calls. "Any change?" we ask each other. She's still saying incubate to describe the tube in her mother's throat. I am still not on a plane. I close my phone.

Stephanie says, "We'll get you home."

*

My mom, Grandma, baby brother, and I visit my aunt and uncle and skinny boy cousins in Albuquerque. Sal and I are the same age. It's spring break for Mom and me, but cousins are still in school, and everyone has to work except Aunt Rita who was smart enough to get the day off from the phone company, so she's taking my mom to Price Club and Dillard's where she loves the sales, but my mom says even with the discount, it's too expensive by rubbing her thumb against her other fingers like she's holding an empty wallet. They dropped Sal and me here at our uncle's house where there is a quiet room for Grandpa to sleep without a bunch of kids running around. That's what Grandma says when I ask why they're not staying at Aunt Rita's with the rest of us. I didn't eat breakfast at Aunt Rita's because it's always rush here and rush there. *Get the boys to school, ohmygodsis, if I drop them off late one more time, check Sal's forehead, does he feel warm to you?*

I was supposed to go with them and my baby brother, but now I have to stay with Grandma and Sal, who can't be out shopping when he's home sick, but even I can tell he's faking. He hasn't thrown up once, which is what I have to do if I want to stay home.

Grandma cooks and cleans in the kitchen. It's not her kitchen, but after one day it already has her cigarettes-bleach-burnt tortilla smell. Pots rattle. Water runs in the sink.

My grandpa is here too, but he does not come out of his bedroom. He does not talk to us or eat with us.

Sal and I sit next to each other on the couch watching music videos. We don't get this channel in Deming. No one tells us to change it or turn off the TV, even though my mom probably would if she was here and could see how the guys from Mötley Crüe wear eyeliner and tight leather pants and no shirts under their vests.

The water in the kitchen shuts off. Grandma comes to the living room and stands between us and the television.

"You want a sandwich?" She says it loud enough for both of us to hear, but she's looking right at Sal. My stomach growls. I look at him too, hoping he'll say yes. He can eat whatever he wants. That's what my aunt and mom say when they talk about their younger bodies, eating and eating and never gaining weight and wouldn't it be nice to be that way again? Sal shakes his head. Maybe I should be like him. Maybe I eat too much. Maybe I shouldn't be hungry. But I am hungry. I haven't eaten today.

"Can I have a sandwich?" I ask, looking up at Grandma, the brown and black of her eyes magnified by the U on her glasses.

"You don't get a sandwich. You're too fat," she says. And then she goes back to the kitchen, or maybe she vanishes behind the smoke from her cigarette.

"You're fat," Sal says, laughing at me.

I want to tell him I'm not. But my legs touch when I sit. The elastic on my shorts folds in under my panza. I sit hugging a pillow so no one can see.

"Aren't you hungry?" I ask.

"I had doughnuts this morning," he says.

When my mom comes back, she asks if I ate. I shake my head no.

West / Cihuatlampa | 51

"Why not?" she asks, like it's my fault, like we're at our house and the kitchen isn't guarded. And then Grandma laughs in that way adults do when they did something wrong and don't want to say sorry. "Why didn't you say something, Michelley?" she asks.

I shake my head. I can't answer her. She makes me a sandwich with white bread and ham and cheese slices and crunchy lettuce. She cuts it in two on a plate at the kitchen table. Even though my stomach thunders and moans, makes a fist and punches, and I haven't eaten all day, now the sandwich is fat and the difference between the boys and me and the reason my grandpa won't come out of his room and my dad doesn't live with us and we are here instead of in our own house like a real family.

*

"Unfortunately, that was the last flight that could get you to El Paso tonight," the agent in Albany says, staring at her computer monitor.

"Can you—please," I say, taking a deep breath. My glasses fog. I exhale, loosening the sob that's been stuck in my chest all morning. "I just—I have to—"

"We need to get our friend home as soon as possible," Stephanie says to the agent, her palm between my shoulders. Karen stands on the other side of me, as if to hold me up. "Maybe Albuquerque or Phoenix? How can we make that happen?"

The agent looks up. My friends smile. I wipe my nose with the back of my hand.

"It looks like there's a flight through Minneapolis arriving in Albuquerque around midnight."

Stephanie hands her credit card to the woman.

"You can pay me back when you're ready," she says to me.

I will never be ready.

I do pay her back—the money, the kindness. I come to learn that we give what we can when we can. But here and now I am empty. Or worse, a sieve. Our finances to me have always felt like a thin-seamed garment that might dissolve in wind. I have dreaded registration day, having a red line through my name, a bureaucrat directing me to the other line that terminates at the financial aid table, only to be told I owe more in library fines or unpaid dues than I will ever see in my life. Or worse that there has been a horrible mistake and I never should have been admitted. *I am sorry*, they would say. And then, *You owe us for all we've invested in you.*

One semester into my Master's degree, and I'm already thousands of dollars in debt. Even with my scholarship, I can't afford the program without loans. I do not come from people who save. Debt looks like gift, a way to touch what we've been denied. Why shouldn't we drive reliable cars? Attend the best schools if we've earned a spot? All my life I've wanted a cushion, a deep breath, something to catch me when the car breaks down or my dad quits his job. There's so little room for error, for emergency or misstep, even less for possibility, for dreams. And yet, here I am getting a Master's degree, living on borrowed money, never able to relax into it, dreading that moment when the rightful owner comes to collect.

*

"Hey, Secretary," my grandma said to me. "Bring me all the mail, even the stuff that looks like junk. It should be in the kitchen drawer under the paper towel holder. And the dresser Grandpa uses as an altar. You know, where I keep the account stuff? There's an envelope with numbers. Bring that tomorrow and a new book of checks. Don't let him see you. He gets all...you know," she said, waving her fingers in front of my face, as though this explained his anxiety. "I need more of the cleaner for my dentures. Your mama knows where it is. And bring me some Kleenex. These," she said, flicking the box of hospital tissues with her hand, "are like a porcupine."

The next morning while my grandpa was in the bathroom, I made the sign of the cross on the Sacred Heart Jesus figurine he held every morning kneeling in front of his altar. His prayers had rubbed off Jesus' eyes and hairline, smoothed his nose to a nub. In the bottom drawer there were Visa statements bundled with rubber bands, a box of security envelopes, a stack of old check registers. I found the envelope with numbers written in jagged rows in my grandma's shaky hand. I found a new book of checks under a deck of funeral cards—Saint Francis, Our Lady of Guadalupe, the Blessed Mother. I found unopened packages of white T-shirts and boxer shorts, three plastic rosaries, tube socks with the elastic stretched because my grandpa didn't like his clothes tight, an empty Tic-Tac container, brown shoelaces still in the package, a television remote, a cordless phone, and a white envelope sealed with duct tape. Scrawled in black ballpoint in my grandpa's handwriting, boxy, all caps, TINO'S PAPERS. PRIVATE. KEEP OUT.

I thought of my own secrets, the journal my mom read because she didn't know how to ask about the cloud over me that summer after my two-year volunteer program in Belize. I wanted her to know without my having to tell her. And I wanted her to know on my terms, without having to climb inside me with a flashlight. "Why didn't you tell me?" she asked when we finally talked, when I told her what had happened. She said she was sorry. She cried.

The water shut off. The shower door slid on its runners. Grandpa must be reaching for a towel. At the foot of his altar, Grandpa's secrets thick, pulsing, heavy in my hands.

*

My brother and his boys meet me after midnight in baggage claim at the Albuquerque Airport. It's January 2nd. They drove three hours north from Las Cruces for me.

The boys are sleepy, but also excited and restless in the way preteens get when they're allowed to stay up late and included in family emergencies. The older one hugs me with one arm, a distancing that started when he entered middle school a year earlier. His brother, bigger, but only ten, wraps his arms around me. "Hi Auntie," he says. It's still Christmas break for the boys. My brother has spent the last few days working, checking in on them at home, eating lunch with my parents and grandpa and aunts and uncles at the hospital. He's been divorced for about five years and is in a brief and rare period between relationships.

The conveyor belt spits out suitcases, roller bags, and boxes tied with string. I wait and wait for my suitcase, a black roller like every other black roller. The carousel empties as other passengers claim their luggage, until all that is left is a flattened cardboard box held together with packing tape. It winds along a u-shaped track and back outside, only to appear again. I picture my suitcase far from here, on a runway in Albany or Minneapolis, icy and snow-covered. Or maybe I left it on top of the twin bed in my dorm room or in the back of Stephanie's Volvo. I go to the small office behind the carousel where an airline agent has me fill out a form describing my bag, no ID tag other than a paper one with its elastic band, the one I filled out while Stephanie put her credit card back in her wallet. I won't remember the address or phone number I list. It's hard to know what is home for me.

Home can't be the same house in Deming, the same small town I outgrew in high school. My parents would let me stay forever. But I can't take their kindness, how careful they are with me, speaking slowly and quietly when they ask, *So, what did you do today? Did you go running? I'm thinking of tacos for dinner. Would you like that, mi'ja?* Whatever life I created for myself in El Paso—consulting, teaching yoga, acting, planning a march for the women of Juárez—vanished when I left Bad Boyfriend. Really, it started vanishing the moment we got together. Like the mountains of Juárez in a dust storm, maybe my life is still there, but from where I stand on this side of the border, I can't see it.

They want me to be well and have no idea how to give it to me. I want to be well. But more, I want to know it's okay I am not. I want someone, anyone, to say, *This is not who you are. This is not permanent. You are still in there.*

Finally outside, I take a deep breath filled with the exhaust of cars idling in the loading zone. My hands sweat inside my gloves. For the first time all day, ski jacket feels too thick, too heavy.

"I parked in the long-term lot on accident," my brother says. He carries the saddlebag with my laptop.

"Aunt Michelle, are you hungry? Dad says he's gonna buy us hamburgers."

*

In the days leading up to her lung surgery, Grandma cooked a pot of beans and a brisket. She made red chile and fresh tortillas. She wrote Grandpa's drug names, dosages, and times of day in blue pen on a sheet of legal paper. She never made a task list but always knew what had to be done. Her pleasure came not from small steps, but from the whole: rinsed yellow Rubbermaid gloves drying on the lip of a blue bucket under the sink, an empty white garbage bag in the trash can, vacuum cleaner lines on the living room area rug, lemon Pledge perfuming every wooden surface from the door pull on the hall bathroom linen closet to the walnut china cabinet against the back wall in the living room.

She shredded the brisket, spooned the beans and red chile into gallon bags and packed them in a cooler with flour tortillas, chopped green chile in an old margarine container, string cheese, dried apricots, Ensure for my grandpa, sliced apples and oranges, and snack packs of chocolate, vanilla, and tapioca pudding. It was the last meal she prepared for us, and she did it because she knew her surgery the next morning would take hours, and we would get hungry, and just because she was getting her lung out didn't mean we "should have to eat that shitty hospital food."

*

The boys prop their pillows against opposite windows in the back seat.

"Sleepy?" I ask.

"No, just getting comfortable. We're gonna stay awake," the older one says.

My brother slams a can of Red Bull and stretches his arms to the night sky. He gets in the truck as I'm taking off my ski jacket.

"I'll keep you company."

I loosen the laces on my hiking boots. My long johns sag around my waist and knees.

He turns the key in the ignition. The Río Grande and her bare cottonwoods carve a black strip into the band of city lights. We cross over the river at Isleta Pueblo. Cold moon on the water. The boys fall silent, their breath steady, reassuring.

I want to sleep. And I feel shame for wanting. I haven't been here keeping vigil at the hospital. I don't have children to care for. I didn't drive hours to get here only to have to work tomorrow. I left for school. And now I am here needing so much—food, a ride, a change of clothes.

*

"A strong gust could sweep our car off the road," my brother said as we approached the sign with flashing lights. *Warning. Vehicles with trailers reduce speed.*

We were going back to Deming from Albuquerque. My mom drove.

"What about the guardrail?"

"See how the windsock is flapping around?" he asked, pointing at the orange fabric attached to the highway sign. "That's actually good. The worst is when it's straight, like it's at attention. You never want to be next to a semi when it's like that. The higher up the vehicle, the easier it is for the wind to pick it up."

My mom took a hand off the wheel to make the sign of the cross. She switched lanes at the lowest point of the road, hovering over the dotted line.

"Now she has more room to maneuver," my brother said. "Just in case."

"In case what?" I asked.

"Wind," my mom said.

"Look at the white lines leading out of the canyon," my brother said. I looked straight ahead. "Whatever you do, don't look over the guardrail."

*

Maybe we save every important conversation for the car. Not a kitchen table, not a park bench or a coffee shop. Maybe what helps is the motion or the promise of an end point, knowing once the vehicle stops and the engine stills, we open the doors, release, and whatever was captured becomes part of something bigger.

Our conversation is long behind us. Another will come years from now, my grandma long gone, my first book out in the world.

I was twenty-three and had been back from Belize for a year. He was turning thirty and divorcing the mother of his children. Some weekends I'd drive from Albuquerque to Las Cruces and stay with my soon-to-be-ex-sister-in-law and the boys she shared with my brother. I should have chosen my brother, but he was the one leaving, and he couldn't say why, only *I don't love her the way a man should love his wife*. I didn't understand how he could be a leaving man, how he could do to his family what our dad had done to us. And I felt a strange kind of responsibility for him blowing up his life. I had worked alone—therapy, *The Courage to Heal*, spiritual direction, a curandera, writing, yoga. What if I had confronted him? What if I had said, *I forgive you*? I couldn't. I didn't.

On one of my visits, one of those afternoons I sat on the couch in the living room that used to be his, he invited me to breakfast the next day. He took me to Village Inn, then drove to Mesilla because it was quiet, a good place to talk. He parked under an oak tree in the lot next to his son's grade school. We stayed in the car, seatbelts unfastened, his window cracked open. We faced a dry cornfield across the street.

"I'm so sorry," he said.

In group therapy the other women told stories of stepfathers, uncles, grandfathers, and dads. They were estranged. They hated the men who hurt them.

My brother was twelve years old when it happened. My brother was a boy.

I nodded, wiped my cheek. I picked at a dry cuticle. His car was spotless, as long as he'd been driving. Even after having kids, the mats were always vacuumed, the dash wiped down with Armor All.

He shook his head, rubbed the pad of his index finger against his thumbnail like a polishing stone. His nails, yellowed, would never fully recover from a fungus that hit in his teens when he'd gnaw and pick them down to the beds.

"It was wrong. What I did. You were a little girl," he said, staring at the steering wheel.

The cornstalks in the field across the street were bones, rows of skeletons yellow as teeth. The farmer would turn these shells back to earth. Or maybe burn the stalks to ash. I had been of bone. A stalk. Woman of ash. Horrible things are done to children. One of those things was done to me. And here, next to me, was the person who did it. Saying he's sorry. Saying it's his fault. I thought of the women in my group, the one whose mother blamed her for what her stepfather did, the one whose uncle died before she could ever confront him. For years I wanted to ask him why, as though he had an answer, as though the answer might heal me. But it was never why that mattered, but who and what, that and it.

I looked in my brother's eyes, milk chocolate shaped like candy footballs we'd buy summers at the tiendita between sessions at the Deming Municipal Pool. Our skin those summers was wet mud. He and I competed to see who would get darker. He had the thickest black hair and was the only one of us with dimples, deep indentations in the middle of his cheeks. He wasn't smiling, but I could trace the lines from his jaw, his chin a tremor. He blinked. I had never seen him cry.

"I know," I said, taking a deep breath. "I know you're sorry."

He nodded and bit his bottom lip. I didn't touch him, didn't put my hand on his. It's not that I didn't want to. My brother was a high wire pulled too tight, the lines on his jaw, his nervous laugh. He had retreated into himself, his shame a hard and solitary thing no one could touch. He had served his penance without my asking, always coming to my rescue.

Picking me up in Albuquerque at midnight. Coaching me through Calculus my senior year of high school. When I emptied my El Paso apartment and moved back to my parents' house, he showed up with boxes and packing tape. I had tried to move with my hands, wrapping dishes in sweaters and kitchen towels and carrying stacks to my car.

There's being the sister who was abused. And there's being the brother. Watching your sister buckle time and again over a breakup, a car accident, a simple move from her apartment to the house where we grew up, wondering how she might have handled life differently if he'd never touched her. Holding his breath through those periods when she seems happy, hoping they will last the same way we hoped my grandma would come back to us.

*

I fell asleep. Of course I fell asleep.

*

When I wake, the truck is pulled over. My brother's seat is empty, the door closed. In shadow behind the truck he does jumping jacks. He shakes out his hands and loosens his neck like a boxer before the fight.

I imagine us over Nogal Canyon on the dangerous crosswinds stretch of highway suspended above the valley floor, the bottom dropped out from under us.

I don't know if our grandpa built this section of highway, but I picture him walking this bridge in his hardhat and orange vest. Its high beams anchored on the floor of La Cañada Alamosa, divided by an arroyo holding only the memory of water. I picture him harnessed to the brace, not looking down, drilling and hammering like a meditation, the hot asphalt up the hill like incense. I picture a canyon littered with piles of metal, oversized loads, moving vans, a motorcycle, the mirror broken off and blinding in the sun.

"Sorry," I say when my brother opens the truck door.

"Don't worry about it," he says. "Just got a little sleepy."

He opens another Red Bull.

"I'm awake now," I say, sitting up and adjusting my jeans and thermals.

"You want some?" he asks, offering me the can.

"I've got water. Thanks."

I scrape the dry skin off my bottom lip by rubbing it against my teeth. I drink the entire bottle, remembering a fountain when I changed planes in Minneapolis, the only water I've had all day.

*

Out my window, at the Las Cruces city limits, the Robledo Mountains sleep like a woman on her side, the folds of flesh in her back warm and motherly. I picture long strands of her hair as the acequias ribboning through cotton, alfalfa, and chile fields, dry until spring when the conservancy district opens the water's flow.

My brother calls our mom from his cell.

"She says she'll meet us outside."

"Did you wake her?"

"Sounds like she was already up."

We pass the water tank with a mural of Juan de Oñate's party forever crossing Jornada del Muerto, a ninety-mile stretch of desert in which the Caballo Mountains and her sisters block access to the Río Grande, the most reliable water source along the Camino Real. I imagine the mural captures the soldiers and priests, families, and livestock early in their journey, before thirst and the feeling that God is distant has settled over them. I imagine them never finding their way or settling in Socorro, a town they named for help, where the river and shelter return, never reaching Acoma Pueblo, bodies and lives on that mesa left intact.

A friar in cassock and sandals guides a woman on a donkey. A headscarf shields her hair and face. The friar looks at her. She looks down at the reins in his hand. Conquistadors ride in front of and behind them.

He is a priest, but I think of them as the Holy Family. I imagine her pregnant like the mother of Christ, no one to take her in. They circle the tank, in search of water.

A cardboard box circles the baggage belt at the Albuquerque Airport. Maybe we all walk in circles.

We spirit past Walmart, Target, the mall, their empty parking lots and streetlamp islands of amber light, past the Golden Corral steakhouse where my grandpa likes the all-you-can-eat buffet. *Mi'ja, pudding. You want some?* My brother steers us off the interstate to the Sleep Inn where my mom waits for us in the parking lot.

My brother gets out of the truck. He hugs our mother and kisses the top of her head. I watch them through my brother's open door, wishing we could all stay exactly as we are, me arriving but not yet here, the boys asleep in the backseat, the diesel engine gurgling, my grandma suspended.

My brother lets my mom go. I open my door.

*

When my mom hugs me, her body feels like a sack of loose flour, the shape shifting depending on the space it fills. Her clothes are too big. They always have been. I don't know my mother's real shape, but I've often imagined her spine is made of caliche, neither dirt nor rock, but something in between that supports the fine dust, gravel and water of her body. Her back is straight, her jaw tight, and even my grandma's death won't break her. I will see her tremble only once years from now when she tells me how much she misses her mom. "She wasn't perfect, but I loved her." My mother will want me close, she will cling to me, a life raft. She will ask me to fix what I did not break. "We need to talk," she will say. She will ask me to make things right. I will leave. And years will pass and only my dad will say, "Come home." She will raise her voice, never yell, because she is upset, never angry. "You talk like nothing good ever happened to you in this house." My dad will put his hand on hers to quiet her. And she will stop. The quiver will begin at her lip and travel down through her jaw and neck, and I will imagine hard clay splintering off her back.

"And your bags, mi'ja?" she asks as we step out of our embrace.

I shake my head and sigh.

West / Cihuatlampa | 61

"It might come in on the next flight," my brother says.

He hugs me goodnight.

"Thank you," I say.

"No problem. See you tomorrow."

"In a few hours."

He chuckles, mostly to himself. He gets back in the truck, closes the door and waves goodbye as he pulls out of the parking lot. Normally, we honk twice when we drive off, but it's three in the morning, my grandma is dying, and my mom looks too tired for loud gestures of endearment.

I have my dad's eyes, but my mom's dark circles and bags. So often we look like we've been punched by tiny fists in our sleep. People tell us we look tired even when we're rested. I imagine a soldier must look this way after days of endless fighting, interrupted sleep, constant motion to a place he doesn't know. I don't know what it is to fight. I don't know what it is to lose my mother. One day she will pass on, and maybe in the lead up to that day, I will stand in a dark hotel parking lot and receive my own children as they come to say goodbye to their grandmother. When that day comes, I am afraid I won't have done enough for my mother, with her. What is left? What do I owe?

Behind her, across the highway, the hospital glows, alive, waiting.

There's nothing to put in her car. Only me with the clothes I've been wearing for sixteen hours and my laptop, so many words, in the saddlebag strapped over my shoulder.

At the hospital, my mother and I stand across from each other, my grandma's bed like an elaborate table between us.

My mother takes her mother's hand in hers and says, "Mama, Michelle's here."

62 | Vessels

Grandma China wants me to have a husband and kids before she dies — and she's not even sick yet

There was this woman in church today, Michelley. She looked just like you, pero she was beautiful, her hair was long and she wore makeup. And I told your grandpa, *Michelle would look pretty if she wore lipstick.*

When I tell Grandma I broke up with the Chicano attorney who wears gray ropers every day (even with business suits) and combs his mustache like Emiliano Zapata

Good. I didn't like him. He was too Mexican.

Last morning of the family reunion (during which my sister-in-law and two cousins announce their pregnancies) Grandma China corners me in her kitchen as I'm serving myself a bowl of menudo

Michelley, when are you gonna have a baby?

You don't need a husband.

Just get pregnant.

When I tell Grandma I broke up with Bad Boyfriend because he's kinda mean and drinks too much

Already? Ooooh… What are you gonna do now?

Home after having her cancerous lung removed, Grandma catches Grandpa slouching

Stop walking like an old man.
Look at him, Michelley.
You'd think I was already dead.

Back in critical care with pneumonia, Grandma reacts to her post-pneumonectomy treatment plan

Four chemos.
Not bad.

She's not supposed to talk during oxygen treatments, so instead Grandma turns over the tissue box on her rolling table and writes a note to Mom, Grandpa and me

Feel 90% Better
Thank our Lord & Family
Doctores y Hospital staff
Love
Mom

acute

(of disease) brief and severe

Our last conversation

You know we're proud of you, right?

What I thought but didn't say

Sometimes.

Earth Shoe
long before

I'm a college freshman home for winter break. My grandma drives me one afternoon to the mall in Las Cruces to buy a pair of winter boots. We pass JC Penney where my parents have credit.

"There's nothing good in there," she says.

Earth Shoe sells the kind of shoes the boys on Dead Poets Society wear, the kind with good leather, no-slip tread, and lots of arch support. I've never bought anything here. My shoes come from KMart or Penneys, or if it's a special occasion, one of the other shops in the mall with big end of season clearance sales so I have to wait until the weather changes to wear them. The lady worker is built like a runner. She has skinny arm muscles and no belly fat. She asks if we're looking for anything in particular.

"I need some comfortable walking shoes I can wear with everything, dress up or dress down."

"It's cold at Harvard."

"Grandma—"

"She goes to Harvard," she tells the saleswoman, "so she needs warm boots."

The saleswoman smiles at me and says, "Congratulations," before leading my grandma to the far wall where the boots and other regular priced shoes are displayed.

I walk to the sale rack, the rack I look for in every clothing store. I pick up a pair of brown loafers. They're sturdy, solid. They go with jeans and black, and maybe even tights and a skirt.

The woman gives me a thick sock to try them on. They fit perfectly.

"Grandma, we can get these," I say.

"She needs to try these in a nine," my grandma says, holding a leather boot with wool lining around the ankle. It looks softer than my bedroom slippers but like I could fight fires in it. The sales lady comes back with my size.

"You're lucky we have these in stock. They're really popular."

West / Cihuatlampa | 73

I've never worn a more comfortable shoe. I walk around the store, imagining Harvard's cobblestone paths under my feet, imagining the daughters of diplomats and presidents wearing shoes like this.

"These are really nice," I say.

"Do you want me to box them up for you?"

"Just the loafers," I say, handing her the sale shoes I can wear until the worst of winter hits, and even then, maybe layer with tights and wool socks.

"She'll wear the boots out of the store," my grandma says, handing the lady her Visa, the one that gets her frequent flier miles on American Airlines.

"Grandma, you don't have to do that."

"You can't be walking around Harvard with ugly shoes. Your mama and daddy worked really hard, so what good is it gonna do for you to get sick and die because your feet are cold? You need warm boots, I'm gonna buy you warm boots. This is my money, and I can do whatever the hell I want with it, and if I wanna buy my granddaughter nice shoes that's what I'm gonna do."

74 | VESSELS

Santos
long before

My grandpa begins and ends each day kneeling on a throw rug before the saints, rosaries, candles, prayer cards, crucifixes, and palms of Sundays past crowded on his dresser. His children and grandchildren bring him santos from the places we have visited or lived. The y-shaped, mahogany, almost feminine cross from Belize, the Divine Child of Prague, a glass-beaded rosary blessed by Pope John Paul II. He lights a devotional candle to Our Lady of Lourdes every morning. A beam of light shoots from her hand to the flowers at her feet. The dresser stands against a wall where he's created a backsplash of Catholic devotion, the Last Supper, a wood and brass crucifix from my grandma's funeral, the story of Saint Frances Xavier Cabrini taped under her black and white photo. On my grandpa's altar, Santo Niño de Atocha sits in his red velvet cape, a basket of bread at his feet. A paper cup filled with sacred earth blessed on the grounds of Santuario de Chimayo spills onto blue-eyed Mary and Joseph. A white ceramic crucifix, split from shoulder to opposite rib as if by lightning, lies flat. I prefer this broken Jesus, how his wounds make him more like us.

Guadalupe watches over them from the wall. Her hair is covered with a blue rebozo. The stars in the fabric hold the last twinkle of night as the sky transitions to dawn. Her hands are together, the palms parted toward her, in prayer. An oval brooch with a black cross in the center rests in the cup of her breastbone. She is surrounded by the sun's rays.

I visited her shrine in Mexico City for the first time when I was twenty-four. I'd expected a chapel with earthen walls and the low light of candles, pilgrims offering prayers from wooden kneelers. In the courtyard, indigenous boys sold rainbows of chicle from cardboard boxes shoelaced around their necks. Dozens of men stood in makeshift stalls hustling photos with plastic donkeys against a Guadalupe backdrop. The Basílica was as big as any arena, incantations echoing off the rounded walls, priests in their uniforms. I didn't know where to find her. I walked along the wall, trusting that the circular shape of the building would lead me to her. The tilma was mounted behind the altar. Four moving walkways ran below her. There was no way to be both still and close to her. I stepped on the walkways again and again, each time taking in a different detail, the way she looked down, eyes almost closed, as if holding a secret, the darkness of her hair, the arrangement of stars on her cloak.

I wanted my own Guadalupe to accompany me back home to New Mexico, where I had returned after college and a volunteer program in Belize. I bought three Guadalupes, one for me, one for my mom, and one as a backup gift for a faithful relative or friend.

In the days since my Grandma China died, my grandpa has added a photo of her from their fiftieth wedding anniversary, the same one we used for her obituary, which, laminated, leans against a clear plastic bottle of holy water from El Santuario.

When my brother and sister-in-law told my grandparents they were getting married, my grandpa made the sign of the cross on each of their foreheads. My grandma wiped her eyes and said, "Let's have a shot." She poured a round of Jack Daniel's from the fifth she kept in the cabinet under the kitchen sink. Over the years, we brought her rum from Belize, pisco from Peru, Mexican tequila. My flight attendant aunt never visited without a plastic bag of airline miniatures.

My grandma didn't like the new priest at Saint Ann's or the one before him, so she stayed home most Saturday evenings while my grandpa went to Spanish Mass. She prayed, not like my grandpa at an altar, but lying down in bed, before she went to sleep. She told me this after her lung was removed and she was recovering at home with a portable oxygen tank she would wheel from room to room. She sat on a rocking chair, a blanket over her knees, a plate of quelites, enchiladas, and beans almost untouched on the tray table in front of her.

"I used to stay up for hours," she said between breaths, "worrying and praying for all of you." She brought the mask up to her nose and mouth, drawing on it the way she once dragged on cigarettes when I was a little girl. "After that September eleven, híjole," she said, scooping beans onto her fork and bringing it up to her mouth, holding the mask to the side of her lips with her other hand. "What if your auntie," she said, wiping her lips with a paper napkin. Oxygen. "Has to work on a flight that crashes?" Bite. Oxygen. "What if some kid." Bite. Oxygen. "At your momma's school." Oxygen. "Takes a gun?" Bite. Oxygen. Napkin. "What if Michelley." Oxygen. "Gets raped. In Belize." She sipped water from the glass on her TV tray. "I couldn't sleep." Bite. "I'd be up all night. Worrying." Oxygen. "Finally, I says to God." Bite. Oxygen. "You take care of them." Oxygen. "Everyone. My whole family.

"¡Hijo! Can you imagine having to eat like this?"

The night she died, my mom, my aunt and I emptied the contents of her black purse onto the kitchen table. Inside was the plastic baggie she used as a wallet. While my mom and her sister took turns spraying her Estee Lauder sample perfume and applying her lipstick, I opened the baggie. Credit cards for JCPenney, Dillards, Service Merchandise, Costco, American Airlines, Visa. Salt packets. The card from her mother's funeral. And prayers loosened from a matchbook-sized devotional. The binding had come undone and the prayers of Saint Francis, Saint Anthony, Saint Jude, and the Blessed Mother mixed in with sugar packets and Winners Club IDs from Sunland Park and Isleta Casinos. I found the book's black cloth binding and pieced together the pages.

I think of my own altar, a steamer trunk in the corner of my parents' guestroom. I think of creating an altar with someone else, a lover, and how I've always kept something hidden, a pebble turned between my fingers or placed in my shoe. I've prayed rosaries, attended daily Mass, offered novenas to Saint Jude for my grandma's recovery. Saint Jude, patron of lost causes, the saint abuelitas pray to so their granddaughters won't still be señoritas when they're my age.

It's not like I saw a faith in my Grandma China others failed to notice. I never heard the prayers she whispered into her pillow at night. I had brought the extra Guadalupe from the Basílica as a backup gift. But her birthday came, and I had nothing. I thought she wouldn't like it or she might ask why I'd given her Grandpa's gift.

She unwrapped it, pulled it from the brown paper covering, held it in front of her with both hands, as though admiring an expensive piece of jewelry.

"A santito. Mi'ja. Thank you."

When I hugged her, I heard her suck in her breath, felt the slightest tremble in her shoulders.

"No one ever brings me santos," she said. "They give them to your grandpa. All I ever get is alcohol."

Acute Respiratory Distress Syndrome (ARDS)

The mortality rate associated with ARDS is 30-40%. If ARDS is accompanied by sepsis, the mortality rate may reach 90%. Median survival is about 2 weeks.

Many patients who succumb to ARDS and its complications die after withdrawal of support.

Mañanitas
that day

Spines of morning sunlight cut through the broken glass tops of the Organ Mountains, pricking my fingers as I massage Grandma's hand. Her skin feels like fallen cottonwood leaves after a winter storm, an infinite mosaic of cells I could rub off with my touch. I work my way up her arm, avoiding the IV and the yellow green bruises where her veins caved under needles.

I can't see it today, but I know a bedsore stains her back. It's hard to think of the sore as part of her, like the mole on her neck. I imagine the sore as bloodletter. Or a portal I might enter and live inside her rib cage where her lung used to be, protected by her bones, expanding her chest with my own breath.

I think she can still hear me.

"Please don't go."

Last night mom and I spent a few hours on fold out chairs next to her bed and left when the room was still dark to shower in my parents' hotel room. My suitcase is still in transit somewhere between Vermont and the Albuquerque airport, or between the airport and Las Cruces, so I'm wearing my cousin's khakis, sneakers, and sweater and the reserve underwear I always pack in my carryon.

"Please."

She hasn't opened her eyes or spoken for three days. It's hard to remember her without the tube in her throat, her tongue swollen and stuck to that tube, her lips parted, cracked. I don't know if she's thirsty. I don't know what she feels, or if. I miss her voice: cigarettes and caliche, Jack Daniel's, red chile and a rolling pin, the tumbleweeds she'd spray paint Christmas white, *hijo de la patada* and *the hell with him*.

"We're not ready."

I brush her hair; it greases my fingers. The tips are honey wheat, but her roots have grown out in a cement shade that withers in the fluorescent panel light above the bed.

I lift the blanket from her feet and calves. Her toenails are thick on her long, wide feet. I moisten her with shea butter, massaging her shins. She hasn't stood for days. She will wobble. Her skin. Skin like parchment. Skin like aspen in winter. Rice paper skin. I rub between her toes with my thumb and forefinger, circle my fists against her arches.

She sleeps on white sheets. Her body is a boy now, breasts sunken into ribcage. I lift one of her legs, and the light settles on her near-bare pubis.

She can't cover herself anymore. Her body belongs to all of us.

"Please send love," I whisper, as though she were a chapel. I want to know love when I see it, to run from it when it's wrong. She met Bad Boyfriend when I took him home to Deming for Easter. We drank manzanilla at her kitchen table. She pulled me aside and said, "I like this one."

So maybe she isn't the best person to ask for help. But my petition is pure. I ask with more faith than I've ever asked for anything. She is a bridge, lying still and quiet on the border between life and death, one hand on this side touching mine, another touching God. In the hours before death, the body shuts down and the spirits return—her mother, the baby boy she lost to pneumonia, all the saints in the prayer book she carries in a plastic baggie in her purse. We'll find it tonight when she is gone, and my aunt, my mother and I empty her purse on the kitchen table, as though some still living part of her remained in there.

I turn off the light.

My breath feels shallow. I put one hand to Grandma, one to me, and smile at the steady rhythm of her heartbeat, wittingly fooled and comforted by the machine's regularity. I sing Las Mañanitas, a song for birthdays and Mother's Day, a song for la Virgen de Guadalupe. I lean over to kiss her forehead. I have to hurry. My cousin, grandpa, and uncle are outside the room. They enter as I sing, "despierta." Wake up.

*

"Would you look at that, Daddy?" Uncle Joe says, pointing to Grandma's lung saturation monitor. "She's at seventy-five," he says, tugging my grandpa toward him by the elbow.

Grandpa Tino smiles for the first time since doctors sedated my grandma and put a tube down her throat three days ago.

"Oh, she had a good night," my grandpa says. "Gracias a Díos."

They embrace. My uncle pats Grandpa's back as they pull apart. The respirator sighs, as if in disbelief.

My Physician Assistant cousin and I stand across Grandma's bed from them. He says, "That's a better number. But she's still not getting enough oxygen."

They don't seem to hear him, their eyes fixed on the monitor.

"I'm concerned her saturation rate is still below eighty."

They continue studying the monitor, as though Chris and I aren't here, as though Grandma doesn't have a tube down her throat, as though by sheer will and attention, they can push the number up past eighty and bring her back to us.

"She's not absorbing nutrition."

"But they're feeding her," my uncle says, finally turning to face us and gesturing toward the feeding tube.

"They are. But her body can't process it. She needs to be absorbing more oxygen." He reaches for our grandpa's hand.

Our uncle puts his arm around Grandpa's shoulder. He's a younger, broader hill than my grandpa, the same baked earth color, but smooth, their hairless faces almost shiny.

Grandma's chest rises and falls in the space between us.

Chris takes a deep breath and says to our uncle and grandpa. "The woman lying here," he says, "is different. She's changed. She's not the person we know."

"I haven't heard any of this from a doctor," Uncle Joe says, setting his coffee on the wheeled table with Grandma's tissues and glasses, his arm still around my grandpa. "You're not a doctor."

I follow Chris out of Grandma's room, through the automatic doors of the critical care unit, and into the corridor. We stand under a curved mirror that sees around corners.

"Her body's shutting down," my cousin says, putting his hand on my shoulder. He is taller than I am, with broad shoulders and a smooth ash-brown face. The warmth from his palm feels solid and steady, something to guide me out from under the mirror and along these white tiled corridors. "Her lung is hardening, like scar tissue."

I nod like I understand what he means, but I don't, or I understand some, enough to know she's going to die, even though I don't know exactly why and how. I draw a deep breath, my spine lengthens, my shoulder swells beneath his hand with something like pride. He is part of this medicalized world. He knows what the doctors have yet to say out loud. He could tell anyone—our grandfather, his mom, my brothers and their wives—but he chose me. I can handle it.

He is late twenties to my early thirties. Above our heads, the mirror hints at a bald spot, a thumbprint on his crown.

The door to critical care opens, and my grandpa walks toward us.

Chris's eyes meet mine. She's not getting better. She's not going home.

Grandpa hardly lifts his feet when he walks. I imagine his orthopedic shoes wearing grooves in the floor tiles. His jacket swishes against his slacks. The sleeves of his windbreaker hang past his wrists; he shrinks each day my grandma is not home, walking these white halls with a hat in his hand. The hat is grey tweed, a green feather tucked in the band. The feather's eye is red on his palm. The upturned brim is an open mouth. I have no alms, no bread to offer, no wine-dipped reed to wet his lips.

It's odd to see him alone. Now and moving forward we will have to take turns maintaining him the way my grandma did. Does. I don't know how to talk about her. She is neither past nor present tense, but somewhere in between.

Grandpa blinks his eyes, tiny caves carved into the clay of his face, Huasteco cheekbones. His body is made of borderlands, Tejas, Nuevo México. His body is El Paso's hills that wind and years reduce to mounds of dirt, his windbreaker a tarp to dull erosion. He jerks his head, a side effect of antipsychotic meds that either saved his life or drained it from him, maybe both. And I wonder in a way I could never say out loud if the cracks in him are part of the reason my grandmother is dying in critical care, sleeping, resting, not fighting hard enough to be with us. And yet, I don't know what I expect her to do with her one lung full of smoke, what to do with her high cholesterol, her tired feet. Maybe she can't hear us at all. Maybe she wants us to solve our own damn problems. Maybe there is no spirit, no will at this point, maybe it's just science, systems. I thought nothing could defeat her. I thought she'd live forever. We all did.

*

At the new hospital across town there's a coffee cart in the main lobby. When my grandpa had quadruple bypass there nine months ago, we drank lattes and cappuccinos with leaf and heart patterns in the froth. We are at the old hospital because this is where the lung specialist has privileges. Here a vending machine dispenses lukewarm silt, like the first summer rains through an arroyo, minus the welcome smell of water in the desert. There's a party size coffee maker on a counter in the consultation room between the reception desk and the security door. There's a canister of white sugar and another of powdered creamer next to the coffee maker. The room is usually empty and locked unless a doctor is meeting with a family, like now.

The window above the door handle is a rectangle. My brother and I take turns looking in, trying to read faces and body language, since we can't read lips, trying to appear as though we aren't spying. Behind the window glass the lung specialist with wire rimmed glasses and Grizzly Adams hair sits across the table from my Physician Assistant cousin. My mom, her siblings, and my grandpa sit around my cousin with his squared shoulders, his gaze focused right on Grizzly.

"We're so useless," my brother says, his eyes on Chris, who's speaking now, looking like a doctor delivering bad news or a sea captain leveling with his crew that their ship is sinking. "What would I do? Bust into the room and say, 'Never fear. The trombonist has arrived.'"

"The trombonist—we're saved!" I say, throwing my arms around my brother and clinging to him like a life raft. We laugh as I release him, as I say something about using my creative writing skills to restore our grandmother's health, as we both wonder out loud why we pursued advanced degrees in our respective crafts. Our time will come later, but sooner than we'd wish. I will write our grandmother's eulogy on behalf of the grandchildren. Together, we grandchildren will decide that he, as the eldest grandchild, should deliver it. Later still, years from now, after my book and the long silence between us, our grandfather's final moments will bring us back into each other's lives, and once again, I will write, and he will read. And later still, he and our other brother will play a trombone duet at my wedding. We give our medicine when we can, how we can.

Grizzly looks at his hands resting on the table, his fingers like a ribcage. He speaks, and then looks up at my family and back down at his hands. Days or weeks or months from now, my mom will tell me, "He said it was time for him to get out of God's way."

What must it be like to believe you keep God from acting? That you hold such power, merit such respect?

*

The consultation room door opens. Grizzly leaves. Uncle David says, "Hey, everyone. Let's gather 'round." My brother and I step into the half-circle forming in front of Grandpa, my mom, and her siblings. My mom is the oldest, but my uncle's a lawyer, so he usually does the talking.

"At five this afternoon, if there's no change, Mom's, Grandma China's, machines will be disconnected. At that time, we will meet in the hall outside critical care. We still have several hours, so between now and then, each of us will get a few minutes alone with her. We'll go oldest to youngest, starting with Grandpa."

We don't weep or cry out. Critical care is waiting for what you already know, for medicine and doctors to catch up with what's been in the heart since we got here.

My parents follow my grandpa toward the security door. Dad walks with his hands in his pockets, looking down at the floor. My mom takes short, quick steps ahead of him and reaches back for his hand as they reach the door. I don't know if he takes her hand, but I hope he does, hope he takes it in both of his because he knows she needs this, because he too has lost his mother, because we're not ready, and it isn't fair, and he kind of owes her—for all the shit from so long ago, for the dental hygienist, and the woman we knew from church, for that night he drank too much, for my mom having to tell us they were getting divorced, and then for setting the conditions of their reconciliation and remarriage: they wouldn't talk about it, and the past would stay in the past. For my brothers and their infidelities, their divorces, their broken kids who don't yet know that kids are resilient. I think he knows. Penance. But more than penance, love. Over the years, he, they will love their way back to wholeness. He will organize Grandpa's finances, helping him pay off my grandma's debt, taking him to doctor appointments and lunch at Si

Señor, cooking for him, cleaning his house. Some things do even out in the end.

*

Critical care is the other family holding down the waiting room table with a jumbo bag of Takis, bottles of apple Mirinda, and burritos wrapped in foil. Only two visitors at a time allowed back to each patient's room, and only after checking in with the old white lady attendant who never says please or thank you and has to buzz you in by pushing a button beneath her desk. It's two college football games on two different televisions mounted in corners of the waiting room. It's Grandpa sitting alone in the consultation room, hands resting on the curve of his cane, an empty chair next to him. I sit, touch his hand.

"She's gone," he says, his voice a hiccup.

I want to say she's not gone yet, not completely. It's not yet five o'clock. The machines are still connected. Her heart is still beating. We can still touch her. We can talk and sing to her. But she's gone enough, more gone than she's ever been.

"She's gone, she's gone, she's gone," he says, over and over until the space between the words disappears, "shegone, shegone, shegone, shegone…"

*

Critical care is Tío Joe stepping into the waiting room with eyes red. He's my grandma's younger brother, a giant horse of a man with a hard body and burnt toast skin from years working construction. When I was little, he always brought a girlfriend home from California, all the same kind of dyed-hair lady with colored eyes, wrinkled cleavage, and a voice sandy with cigarette smoke. They called me sweetie or darlin'. They played poker, laughed at my uncle's jokes, talked too loud for Grandma's kitchen. They mixed drinks in Grandma's fancy green-glass glasses with the smoky bottom. One stirred Jack into Coke with a butter knife; another used her chipped pinky fingernail.

Tío once emptied Grandma's brandy and replaced the liquid with weak tea. Nobody noticed until Grandma poured a shot to make bizcochitos. He once passed out on her living room floor, and all the kids had to step around him to get to the screen door we'd run through to get to Grandma's side yard. Tío finally quit drinking. I don't know how it happened, only that it was between visits from California to Grandma's house in Deming and that he went from smelling like stale beer to smelling like Grandpa's Old Spice.

"How you doing, Tío?" my brother asks.

"Aquí, no más."

Tío who's buried two children. One son overdosed. Another shot himself with a harpoon gun in front of his mother. I don't know how he remains upright.

Aquí, no más.

Here, nothing more.

Here, no more.

Here no more.

*

A FedEx driver delivers my suitcase to the hospital entrance. I don't want to wear those clothes. I don't want my underwear or wool socks, my flannel pajamas or saggy jeans. The greys, blacks and browns. In Vermont winter is too much, and here it is not enough. Nothing in this flimsy suitcase could protect me from ice storm, protect me from drought, from a season inside myself, without my grandma.

*

Critical care is one long day and many exactly the same days. I drive Grandpa to State Farm for the life insurance forms we'll need to file when she passes. "Mi'ja, they're gonna ask to send the check right to Baca Funerals, but I'm gonna tell them no because the funeral places use up all the money, and then you pay too much." The insurance office is in one of the houses turned businesses across from the university. When my mom was working on her degree, I'd sometimes come with her and sit quietly while she met with her advisor, a Chicano with a mustache and a collared shirt. His office was full of books. Development in this area took off before the city could update its drainage system and so every summer during monsoon season, cars floated down flooded streets. My grandpa had always told us the brakes could give out if they got too wet, and so my mom and I would wait out a storm under the awning of a bank or furniture store before driving the hour back to Deming. We might eat the bean burritos my mom packed, the just-in-case, you-never-know, so-we-don't-have-to-stop burritos she'd prepare from the permanent pot of beans in the fridge, mashing and frying the beans in cast iron, sprinkling in whatever cheese happened to be in the house, sometimes American slices, sometimes boxed cheese we'd pick up once a month. Once or twice on these trips, we stopped at Lujan's Bakery for pan dulce and the car smelled like warm sugar all the way home. This was before New Mexico State or any university had a branch in Deming, before the internet. If you lived in Deming and you wanted a degree, even if you had four children and a full-time job as a teacher's aide, you had to drive the family station wagon up and down Interstate 10 at least twice a week. After the youngest went to bed, you completed assignments on wide-ruled notebook sheets that your oldest would transform onto onion skin rolled into the electric typewriter your husband borrowed from his office supply job. This is how you became a teacher, how you showed your daughter that education was a ticket out of used cars, borrowed typewriters, and government cheese.

The insurance broker speaks Spanish to my grandpa. I'm grateful for every kindness toward him. He touches Grandpa's hands and hugs him when we leave.

The hospital sits taller than any other building in Las Cruces. It's sand colored and eight stories high atop the east mesa, surrounded by medical clinics, doctor's offices, gas stations, and hotels. I used to like this part of town, when the mall at the other end of Telshor Drive was new, and we got to shop there because my mom had credit at JCPenney. As we pull back into the parking lot, my grandpa says, looking out the passenger window, "I sure hope your grandma don't die. The oxygen, it was good this morning. That's good."

I let his hope fill the space between us, even though we both know the reading on her oxygen meter doesn't matter anymore. We both know her lung is scar tissue, and by this time tomorrow she will be dead. But I let him talk because here inside this white minivan with its foam blue dash mat, beaded wood seat covers, and cushion for my grandpa's lower back, he feels almost at home. We could be waiting for my grandma to come out of the bank or some department store at the mall to load flowered sheets or ceramic angels and apricot potpourri or boxes of Börn sandals and wedge heels from the sale at Dillard's that don't fit her but she couldn't let go for that price.

The van is parked. The engine still. We sit. There should be snow on the Organ Mountains.

"It's good," he says, his half-smile now a quiver.

"Yeah," I say, reaching for the insurance papers on his lap. The sun is directly above the hospital now. A semi downshifts on the interstate below us. It must be my turn to say goodbye.

*

I don't think she can hear me anymore. I don't know what's changed. I hold her hand, run my finger along her knuckles, swollen and hard like the knots of young cottonwoods. I tell her she can go, knowing she doesn't need my permission. A red car passes along the speed zone outside her window. A man in sunglasses walks his dog and smokes a cigarette.

I don't want to be here anymore.

*

In reality, there are many plugs powering many machines. It's not an off-on switch. It's not pulling one plug that ends a life. There's one plug connected to the tubes that feed her, one that breathes for her, another to regulate her heartbeat, one to take her blood pressure, and a monitor to report their findings. These instruments have become the main characters in my grandma's story. They have their own soundtrack, one we will miss: the high pitch when her heart rate slips below a safe level, the oxygen's steady hiss, the blood pressure machine's long sigh.

We don't see how the tubes and needles and waste bag and monitors exit, how the nurses in critical care transition a patient from being to body.

We saw the before: the ambulance that brought her here. The day she stood up and sat down before she could take a step. The oncologist from

India shaking his head. *She should be stronger by now.* Christmas in a regular room on the fourth floor, an oxygen mask over her mouth and nose so she spoke with eyes and touch. I brought her a star shaped candleholder, hand-painted like mother of pearl. She liked the cellophane wrapping, the mesh ribbons in green and red, held up her hand, her palm facing me, when I tried to unwrap it. *Leave it.* She liked new things. It didn't really matter what they were. Back to critical care. Too many visitors in her room. We're supposed to come in pairs, Noah's creatures crossing over water to the ark. There's the tube in her throat so she can breathe. Sedation so she can rest. There's speaking low and family meetings and paperwork and signatures. And there is now, all twenty-something of us lining up single file outside the double doors to critical care so the nurse will know where to find us when they are ready, when the plugs are pulled, the machines rolled out. My mom and aunt leave the line and go into their mother's room to comb her hair and put in her teeth.

A nurse walks by wheeling a tray of peanut butter cookies and a sweaty plastic pitcher of ice water.

My mom opens the door linking Grandma's side of critical care to ours and says, "It's time."

Our long line of family wraps around her bed. Grandma sits up with her back propped against white pillows. Her cheeks are blushed in coral or seashell. She's covered to the waist with a white sheet. The light above her bed is the light of box stores where she'd open charge accounts to get a discount. The curtains are drawn, holding dusk outside the room. Behind the other window, nurse shadows pass along the hall. One steps into our room and whispers, "She can't feel anything, but she can still hear you."

I don't think she can. I think she left sometime this afternoon.

The peanut butter cookies and ice water sit in the corner.

Grandpa stands next to Grandma's bed and holds her hand. My mother stands across from him, weeping like Mary Magdalene at the tomb. Grandpa holds tight to her hand. His eyes are closed, his head nodding down toward my grandma and up toward the ceiling.

"Let go, Mama," my mom says, stroking her mother's hand, kissing her head, as she would an infant.

Each of us rests a hand on Grandma's bed. I touch her feet over the white sheet covering her legs.

When I look up again, Grandma's top dentures have slipped onto her lower lip. She looks like she's grinning. My mom's shoulders tighten beneath her blouse.

"We're all here with you," my mom says to my dying, grinning grandmother. She caresses Grandma's cheek. She moves her face closer to my grandma's, as if to kiss her nose. Then she slides her thumb under Grandma's chin and pushes the dentures up and in Grandma's mouth, all the while cooing, almost chanting, "We're all here with you. It's okay to go." The teeth hold long enough for my mom to turn to her brother and say, "Come." Then they slip. By the time Uncle Joe reaches for his mother's hand, she is smiling again.

He kisses her cheek and strokes her face, pushing up on her jaw with his palm. The dentures sink lower on her bottom lip.

One by one, my aunts and uncles approach my grandma and try to reset her teeth without looking like they're trying to reset her teeth. I inhale and look around the room. My younger brother holds his girlfriend's hand. Their two-month-old baby is in the waiting room with our ex-sister-in-law, who offered to watch the babies and toddlers so we could be with my grandma when she passes. Her own children are here with us, my teenage nephews and niece standing clumped together, holding a space for their father, my brother who's driving in from California. He will arrive too late to say goodbye. My mom extends an arm to my oldest brother.

"Come closer," she says. "Say goodbye."

When it's my turn to say goodbye, I kiss Grandma's hand and her cheek. I finger-brush the hair lying flat against her scalp. Her teeth are completely covering her bottom lip. I kiss her forehead, whisper, "Thank you, Grandma."

My Tío Dindy starts to sing Las Mañanitas, out of rhythm, on his own. He calls out, "Go Carnala."

My mom asks me to recite the twenty-third Psalm. I don't know all the words. I get as far as goodness and kindness when Aunt Rita throws her upper body onto Grandma's bed and cries out, "Mommy. Mommy. Mommymommymommymommymommy."

I lay my palm between Aunt Rita's shoulder blades as her sorrow breaks open, a desert flash flood, the Mimbres River after a rainstorm, water gushing, a river of silt, sandy banks crumbling into the current.

She sobs, and I want her to sob. I wish we all could.

"Let her go, Rita," my mom or uncle or great uncle says, or maybe all of them do.

She pries herself up from the bed to stand and wipes her eyes, the freckles on her cheeks red, her eyes puffy.

"I know," she says quietly, inhaling and then straightening her blouse as she exhales.

I wish she would yell, *Let me do this*. Where is our gnashing of teeth? Our sackcloth and ashes?

I don't want to be here anymore. My grandmother can't hear us. She left sometime during the day, between college football games or as I drove Grandpa to the State Farm office.

I step through the colorless hospital room, around the wheeled cart of untouched cookies and sweaty water pitcher and walk into the hallway. Chris follows and walks to the nurses' station across from Grandma's open door. He speaks their language, looks up at a monitor and nods at the nurse with the snowflake scrubs. She nods back at him. He turns to me and says, "She's gone."

My cousin says the heart has reserves. Without machines, as death nears, it beats slower then surges one last time, a comeback, before it drops to a faint resting pace. Then it stops. My grandma's heart didn't do that. Once the machines were gone, her heart beat slower and weaker until it didn't. She died in thirty minutes. She had nothing left.

Chris weaves through our family to Grandpa, puts his hand on his shoulder and whispers, loud enough for us to hear, "She's gone." Even when Chris leads him out of the room into the hallway, Grandpa says, "She's not gone. She's not gone."

I hold my mother next to Grandma's bed.

"She looks so peaceful," my mom says.

She doesn't. But my mom says this about every body at every funeral, even with their jaws sewn tight, their faces caked in a too-light foundation and a too-pink blush. My grandma's dentures are still stuck on her bottom lip. She's propped on pillows under yellow light.

The room empties. My mom opens the curtains on her way out. The peaks of the Organ Mountains cut open the sky, red sunlight bleeding on desert willow and sage, organ pipe cactus, down the mountain into Las Cruces, onto my grandma, onto me.

North / Mictlampa

rumbo de los antepasados, de la memoria
rumbo de la oscuridad
donde el sol menos brilla

we don't meet
we remember
we met lifetimes ago and

again and again in each

life opening

into this

one

Mamá Malinche

Malintzín, Marina, Malinche was passed from one set of hands to another, all of them rough. Sometimes I can't hear her voice at all. Sometimes her screams wake me.

She tells me her story in Tonantzín's Temple in Tepeyac, en la hoja blanca, through my mother and grandmothers and their mothers.

Today she whispers to me in a temazcal.

Before the Spaniards came, our people bathed in earthen ovens, sweating out all that was impure.

Her voice rises in the rosemary and poleo steam drifting from the hot rocks, through the darkness, to me.

Mothers birthed in these wombs of wet earth. We entered the world unafraid.

Her voice sinks into the earth, moist and dark beneath me. Her voice in the baked adobe bricks around me, this womb where I sweat, where I feel young and weak, as young as she was that morning her mother handed her to traders beneath the silvery leaves of the give-and-take, as weak as she must have felt on that long walk from her istmo to the Yucatán. Her brother the only child in her mother's house, a slave girl dead in her place.

Tlatoani
Malinche

The first morning, Moctezuma's runners, men who shone like Tonatiuh, came to us on foot. Kneeling over metates, my sisters and I ground corn light as the Captain's hair. I could feel the vibration from the stone up through my bones and into my teeth, could almost taste ground corn on my tongue.

"Who is Tlatoani?" Moctezuma's men asked.

The bearded ones stood silent, their confusion and fear prickling my skin.

Tlatoani. He who speaks for his people. They spoke my mother's tongue. I stilled my hands, kept my head down. My sisters ground corn.

They asked again, "Who is Tlatoani?"

Staring at the corn dust and metate, I pointed to the Captain.

"Him," I said, almost feeling my bones powder between mortar and pestle.

North / Mictlampa

Mamá Malinche

I don't remember my name. Is it possible for a man—for a people and a history—to erase you so completely your reflection disappears? Malintzín. Is this my name? I say that word, and it sounds foreign to me. In the hands closed over my heart, I guard the name my mother whispered, my father's love, my language, all things precious. With you, hija, I uncoil a scroll never captured in a codex or on the chalk-eyed men's parchment.

*

I loved my mother's son from the moment he came out of the temazcal. He cried as the light hit his eyes, as his father held him over his head and presented him to the village and the ancestors.

"My son," he said.

"My brother," I whispered, so soft only the servant girl and I could hear.

I moved to see the baby, to see myself in his black eyes. I extended my hand to touch his hair, still wet from my mother's womb. His father placed a hand between us.

"He is not your brother," he said. "You are your father's child."

I learned to look in my brother's eyes only when my stepfather left our home. I learned to listen for the man's heavy steps at the door, to touch the baby one last time before his father filled the entrance, before he sent the servant and me outside to work, to play, to wander, to do anything but be in his presence.

She was a shadow, the servant girl, awake and waiting each morning when I opened my eyes, running a wooden comb through my hair before touching her fingers to her own. She prepared my food, lifting it up to my lips with her brown hands, watching until I finished, and only then turning her back to me as she ate at her mat, quickly, so as not to bore me, so as to prepare my petate for afternoon sleep. I remember the day my father gave her to me, touched his hand to mine as I kneeled beside

98 | VESSELS

the petate where he lay day and night. She will care for you when I am gone, he said. He called her my little mirror. The next morning his coughing stopped, and he returned to the spirits in silence. After the ceremonies, after we removed the mourning cloth from our door, the new man came to our home, placed his mat next to my mother's and soon her belly swelled with his love.

It was still dark when my mother woke me that last morning. She placed a hand over my mouth before I could speak. As I stood, she rolled the servant girl onto my mat. The girl's mat lay rolled and bound at my mother's knees. She placed her fingers over the girl's eyelids and then gathered her long hair and laid it over her face. I shook the girl, not understanding how she could sleep while my eyes were open, how she couldn't sense the shift in my breath through her dreams. She lay still.

"She sleeps for you," my mother whispered. "She lies in your place."

My mother pulled me from the girl. She dressed me. As she combed my hair, she stretched her fingers, shaking her hands as though releasing a weight from within. Each time I opened my mouth to speak she shook her head, silencing me with her eyes. She pulled me from our home by the wrist and led me through the empty paths to the edge of the village. The men who traded skins in the market waited for us beneath the fan-shaped leaves of the give-and-take palm, the spines on its stem reaching toward them, toward me. She placed the girl's bound mat in my hands. She wrapped my comb and cakes of amaranto and maíz in leaves of hierba santa and bound them with three silver hairs plucked from her head of black.

She touched her hand to the give-and-take, pricking herself. Her fingers swelled. Blood flowed from her palm. Then she reached above the spines and cut into the bark with a flint. The tree's insides were pink as the clouds at sunrise. She chewed by bark, then pressed it to her wound. The bleeding stopped. Her color, the sweet brown of cacao seeds, returned. She held my hands in hers, the bark of the give-and-take between us.

"Your joy and your pain are intertwined. The spirits will give you what you need." She pointed to a heart-shaped leaf. "Prepare a tea to clean your blood." She placed the pink bark in my hand. "Heart heals heart." Corazón cura corazón.

She kissed my forehead. "I'll say the girl ran away. You, my daughter, I will mourn until we find one another again beneath the earth."

She held me to her until the men pulled me into the rising sun. As light spread across the valley and I stepped farther away from her, she must have screamed my name, for I felt her sorrow in my own chest. In her scream I heard the wail of death. I walked and understood with each step that I no longer existed as I once had, that there could be only one child in my stepfather's house.

*

I was still a girl when they came to Potonchan, the men dressed in iron with hair on their faces. I was a servant among the Maya, a girl-child, who cooked and slept in the cacique's quarters from the day my blood began to flow.

"Marina," the man in long skirts called out as he plunged me in water. I thought he called the sky. The sun warmed my eyelids in that moment without breath beneath the surface. I opened my eyes as he pulled me up and longed to see my mother's face. I reached for the hands that once held me gently, but my fingers could have more easily held the sun.

"Marina, en el nombre del padre, del hijo, y del espíritu santo."

There were twenty of us. We knew what it was to take a man's body into our own. But this Cristo offered so little of himself, a taste of corn on my tongue. I felt him travel through me, filling me, cross and all. I felt his fingernails scratching from beneath my skin. That night, when the Captain gave me to his friend, it was this Jesus he touched inside me, Jesus whose cross opened and let the hungry man in.

We journeyed soon after.

If I'd loved the Captain I might remember the moment he made me his, how he kept me close as dust. I more remember how the traveling army grew with each falling sun, how more daughters and concubines and servants lay with the iron-dressed men on their sleeping mats.

*

They called me La Malinche. The men who drew our history gave me long black hair and bare feet, dressed me in a white huipil. A scroll hovers above my head, a winged tongue flies from my lips to Moctezuma's ears.

His men couldn't hear how the tongues changed between villages, couldn't see the wide hips of the Chatino women, the narrow shoulders of the Quiché, the bare breasts of the Maya, the flat noses of the Huichol. I spoke the people into being. We were nations—Mexica, Tlaxcala, Maya, Cholula, Yucateca, Huasteca. We were Totonac, Olmeca.

I made our nations more than jade, gold, and the dark skin of the New World. I made us floricanto y maíz, artisans who pounded maguey into fine paper, prostitutes with red teeth, men of science who read fire in the sky, and priests who held beating hearts in their palms.

*

The people named the Captain for me. El Malinche.

*

Moctezuma fell.

Pustules covered Cuitlahuac's skin. He lay in bed until the sickness devoured him.

The Captain's men murdered Cuahtemoc. He died far from home, adrift. His soul sank to the ocean floor and joined all those washed away when the frailes pushed our heads under water and held us until they sliced a cross in the air. México sweeps her children to him in the currents of the Río Bravo. And the women. So many women who die in the desert. It takes them an age to come home. Their bones turn to chalk, to dust blown across the Chihuahuan desert to el Río to Cuahtemoc.

*

I remember the Captain's smell, like the first quail I was forced to kill for his meal. He wanted the fattest of the family that walked with us as the air grew thinner and the mountains of fire closed around us. He didn't notice how it walked with the gait of a sick warrior, how it surrendered to me as I extended my hand. I pulled its skin apart without the Captain's jade knife, with my strong hands opening wider the green wound eating the creature's flesh and dropping its gray feathers along the rocks. Through this opening, the edges rough as corn husks, a single worm burrowed toward the creature's heart. I heaved, but my mouth only warmed and watered.

I held the quail facing me. How normal it looked. Its crown, a hook curled toward me. I closed its eyes.

This is how the Captain smelled to me, like game rotting in his salty sweat, dusted by the paths we cut through each mountain's heart.

*

Men have called us lovers.

The Captain loved me as he loved his horse, as he loved the sheath strapped to his side. He pulled me toward him, not like a woman but like a cloth to wipe his sweat and filth. He always touched my lips first with his coarse fingers. "So full," he said. "So brown and dry from the sun." I imagined someone else there with us, someone he talked to as he handled me. He bit my lips, peeled the dry skin off with his teeth, licked the pinholes of blood. He put his mouth on mine and pushed my teeth open with his tongue. He sucked my tongue. He called it a cord. He only need pull and all he wanted in this land would be his.

And then he talked to me, "When you die, I'll cut your tongue with my jade knife and wear it next to my heart." He looked me in the eyes, pressing his fingers into my jaw, hissing, "Malintzín. Malintzín."

What did I ever own?
Malinche—mamá del mestizaje, del xicanismo

When our son was mine his whole body fit across my chest. By day walking among the men I carried him in a black rebozo. At night, I knotted my hair to hold him in place.
The Captain carried him across an ocean to his king.
He left me only the long black hair I unbraid and drape across these breasts that drip milk each time a child cries.

Mamá Malinche

Malintzín. I close my eyes in the temazcal, feel my body sinking into the warm, wet earth. I entered to sweat her out of me, thinking us impure, to slip from this chain I no longer want to hold.

But it binds our ankles like strangler vines. And when you try to run, you trip, cutting your knees and palms with bits of mirrored glass.

I bleed.

Tell the story with your blood. I am there. You are there with me and when you open, you will birth me. You will birth your own self.

Herencia: Crecencio
bisabuelo—padre de mi abuelo materno Florentino

He's the pink-eared man who slept in the milpa, who looked at her too long when she passed the fields with an empty gourd balanced on her head. One hand steadied the gourd, the other brushed against the tall grasses brushing against him.

When she returned, her skirt's hem damp from the river, the gourd heavier with the family's water, he stood facing her father, and though they were the same height, the new man seemed taller, as though the lightness of his skin had earned him a place in the clouds. As she brought the water to her feet, the man smiled in her direction. Her father nodded, and she understood she no longer belonged to her parents, but to the man.

That night, she sat alone with him beneath the desert stars and crescent moon. He pointed to his chest and said, "Christopher." She stared at the lunares washed across his cheeks and nose like a mask, read them the way elders read the stars. He came from across the ocean. "Christopher Moran," he said. He opened her hand, traced her palm, the veins on her wrist, the way early navigators traced their journeys on parchment maps, sacred texts guiding them home. "Ireland," he said. "Soy Irlandes." He kissed her fingers. She nodded. He put his nose to her neck and breathed her scent—damp earth where the river laps the bank—and she knew the tall grasses, the milpa, her river path, her round hands and hips were now his home.

He breathed words she didn't understand, knelt before her like an offering, and then lowered her back and shoulders to the ground. He parted the folds of her. He gave himself to her, and in the giving, she broke open, emptied. Thirsty, with the ground solid under her back, she drank him, drank the lunares, the stars, the crescent moon.

Through the rains, the river's rise, the harvest and dry season, la medialuna filled her, expanding, kicking, until the night Mother walked her through the milpa and a clearing to the huanacaxtle. Its canopy embraced them as Mother positioned the girl's hands around the rope hanging from its thickest branch. Tiny streams ran down the girl's legs to the tree's well. Its ear-like pods bore witness and received as Mother whispered, "Gracias, Madre," to the tree.

The girl squatted, her sweaty hands fisted above a thick knot. She pushed. Mother knelt at her feet with arms outreached. When the child slipped out of her into Mother's open hands, she expected to see her own reflection, a dark-haired girl with a lazy eye and skin the color of dried leaves. "A boy," Mother said. His face so pale it was almost translucent.

The boy cried. She sat and rested her back against La Madre, her toes in the tree's earth, cooled by her own water. Mother put him against her chest. She stared at this new creature, the moonlight of his face, understood in his cry that for him, she was home. Her round hands and breasts were now his.

Mother buried the placenta beneath La Madre.

The girl, now a mother, would live to wave to her compañero at the train platform, the cars filled with silver from the mountains embracing her home. She would live to feel the lunares on her compañero's face transform to a rash, then to raised bumps filled with liquid, then pus. They would spread to his hands, his arms. By the time they choked his nose and mouth, she would feel them on her own face.

The boy Crecencio would live to watch his abuelo burn the blankets in which his mother once wrapped him. He would sprinkle dirt on their ashes. He would be sent away, hacia el norte, to another river, a coal-mining town named for pain. He would outlive three wives, spend his days in the darkness of a mine. He would live to eighty, and like his father before him, die far from home.

Crecencio y Lute
bisabuelo y bisabuela—padres de mi abuelo materno Florentino

She wasn't the first woman to live in my great-grandfather's house. She was the first to give him children, the first to survive a birth.

"Lute. Eleuteria."

He grunted more than called her name from the porch where he sat Saturday to Sunday dusk emptying the bottle of aguardiente, his fingers closed around its neck the same way they closed around her skinny wrist each time he led her to the back room. He was pale and powerful, freckled, with black hair and eyes like old pennies.

Crecencio Moran. His name was unlike any she'd ever heard. It was the moon beneath la Virgen's feet y el crecimiento, the child growing inside her. Crecer. Creyente y creencia, his name was believer and belief.

He rarely asked anything of her when he summoned her to the porch, only gestured to the groove on the step, worn like the well of a metate from his boots and those of so many mine workers who filled the house and village when coal flowed more freely along the new railroad than las aguas del Río Bravo. She sat with her hands on her belly, her feet in the dirt, and listened as he spit tobacco juice into an empty bottle.

These evenings they did not speak. Inevitably, as the sun left them in darkness, he would tilt his head back and fall to sleep, and she would slip into the house, sprinkling its splintered floor with water droplets to keep from rising the dust beneath their feet.

Crecencio and Lute loved best when my grandfather Florentino was a baby. The family shared a bed, with Lute on her back, Crecencio's head on Lute's chest, and Florentino lying beside them on a rolled blanket. Florentino was possibility, a blossom, his nickname Tino, un botón, a bud. His name was a garden, the shade of cornstalks in the milpa, a resting place, like that space between Lute's breasts, where Crecencio felt like a woman's child, that boy in San Luís Potosí before smallpox took his apás and forced him north to work with tíos who mocked his name and pulled his pink ears. He could sleep in that space, warm his hands, feel his mother's heartbeat, open his eyes and stare full-on at the sun as though it were another compañero's headlamp guiding him through the mine. He could live and die with his head resting on Lute's breastbone, dream of his birth beneath el huanacaxtle, forget his lungs lined with coal dust, all while Lute whispered *Tino-flor-aflorecer-Florentino-floreciente*.

But, like the lives of women, these moments never lasted. Another baby came, Isabel. She suckled the color from her mother's breast, darkened to a baked adobe as her skin dried like cornhusks. Her cries drowned Crecencio's memory until he forgot the beauty of his own daughter's name. Before Isabel could talk, Crecencio began calling her Chavela. The nickname sounded to Lute like drunkenness, like anger.

The last night la partera thrust a new baby into Crecencio's arms, then rushed back to Lute before he could name the sharp metal taste piercing the darkness like the newborn's cries. He fingered the blood on the blanket's hem and knew he held his wife's remaining breaths.

Childbirth is a form of battle, its victims like fallen warriors. The spirits of fallen mothers strengthen soldiers in battle and rise to Cihuatlampa, the place of the women, where all mothers who die in childbirth accompany the sun from zenith to dusk. Their faces turn to bone, their hands to eagle claws, and they descend to earth only as Cihuateteo, bare-breasted and haunting crossroads at night, stealing children, and seducing men.

Lute surrendered.

After the burial, her children scattered like los hijos de La Malinche. Baby Lute to her tíos on the ranch, Chavela y Florentino to a sister in Dolores.

Men from the mine were let go, their homes abandoned to dust and ghosts. And though Crecencio still had a place there, each day the underground shafts felt more like the chambers of a dying heart. He married again. And again. Always outlasting his wives. In my mother's family, the men outlive the women. We die of childbirth, cancer, exhaustion, love.

At dusk, plunging the sun into the Western Ocean, Eleuteria hovers for an instant, a breath, exhaling another day of life across the water, across the borderlands to her tres hijos. Each child shifts to night—Tino flips on the Virgin Mary night light in his wife's empty kitchen, Chavela takes her blood pressure, Lute, named for her dead mother, smokes a cigarette on their father's porch. Eleuteria sinks beneath the earth, pushing the sun to another side of sky.

Casiano y Jesus, who everyone called Susi
bisabuelo y bisabuela—padres de mi abuela materna China

My great grandma left her husband.

Casiano. Susi prayed his name like a rosary, loved it before and after she loved him, before and after kneading her fingers along the wooden beads of his spine.

Casiano sounds like casarse. To marry. He never gave her a ring.

Sounds like cazar. To hunt.

He gave her a place to return when loneliness and longing weighed heavier than fear and their story.

"Ya no puedo," she said when she called China from the white house she cleaned on Tuesdays and Thursdays. China, the youngest of her daughters, all grown up now, married a good man, a Texas boy del rancho. He'd served in the war. He worked. He treated his suegra with respect. They could help her. Between starching her boss's collars and ironing his wife's tablecloths, Susi whispered as though Casiano were sleeping next to her, "Tu daddy va a cazar in the morning. Come for me."

They came in a green pickup while Casiano shot jackrabbits in the Floridas, the blue desert mountains where Susi ran from the shed Casiano built of gutted oil drums, scrap wood, and nails pulled from her boss's barn and outhouse.

China's husband Florentino drove. Before the war, he drove a government truck to Deming from Columbus on weekends, opening the tailgate and letting the CC Camp workers spill onto the streets, darkening downtown with their brown uniforms and black hair. He could have spent another night in the park, covering his bare arms with newspapers, but Susi had felt a tenderness for him, this motherless child, so when he came to her with his head down and asked if she might spare un rinconcito for a poor boy from Texas, she gestured with her chin to the space between the wood stove and the wall.

Today she needed Tino to drive and defend her in case Casiano came back early with bloody jackrabbits in one hand and his shotgun in the other. Her husband would not shoot her. It was never death that frightened her, pero esa rabia that yelled her into shadows, that made him kill the life around her. He shot rabbits they would never eat, held water from tomato plants she resurrected with each return, hacked the ocotillo growing wild outside their door, its petals like red drops on cracked earth.

My mother was a little girl. I remember things I don't really know, things they would tell years later when shame loosened and secrets either exploded or leaked from them—my great-grandma left her husband; Tino was shelled by his own men, por eso he got to come home.

Today China, Susi's daughter, jumped out of the green truck and ran toward Susi before Tino brought it to a full stop, as though she might swoop up her mother and toss her in the truck bed next to Cookie, my mother.

"Take me home," Susi told them, back through town and across the tracks where the Mexicanos and Black folks lived.

China hadn't told her about Tino's sunrise cries *Mamá, Mamá* waking the house, how some days he slept while other men left their homes for work, how each night she hid the kitchen knife from him, wrapping it in an old slip. While he'd lock the doors or pray to the saints gathered on the bedroom shelf, she'd slip the bundle under the stuffed flour sack that was her pillow and rest her head before he lay next to her. He never slept through the night.

My great-grandmother left her husband. We don't ask why. It wasn't the first time, but my mom says it was the last. *He was a drinker*, she says. This is how language recreates us. We say drinker, charmer, womanizer. Not drunk, free-loader. And what is the word for a man who craves women?

Though we have always been here, I call this day her crossing. There are borders other than those between countries, borders between man and woman, sanity and madness, living and dead. These borders shift.

There are rules for visiting the opposite sex, the infirm, the dead. Cross your legs at the ankle, wash your hands in warm water, shake el polvo de los muertos from your shoes, porque si no, the dead follow you home.

There must be rules for returning men and women from battle, for bringing home their souls. Bless a forehead, sprinkle the chest with agua florida, sweep off el susto con un ramo de romero.

We don't know what we carry until it returns to us in our children and their children. And theirs.

I remember Susi's bare feet, China's work shirt tied at the waist, dust rising from the tires and re-settling on her hairnet like mist on a spider web. I remember Cookie riding in back, thinking it was an adventure they were on. Dust on her black curls, her skinny arms that Susi or any man could have snapped like chickens' necks, extended as her grandma climbed next to her in the bed.

They left Casiano hunting rabbits, his shotgun blasts echoing against the mountain, echoing in my Great-Grandma Susi's ribcage. And Tino's. And China's. And my mother's. And mine. As the green truck pulled away, they faced the disappearing shed together, Susi's hand at the nape of my mom's curls, my mom's fingers kneading the beads of her grandmother's hand.

112 | Vessels

Soy Yo
abuelos maternos—China y Florentino

It's dark and he doesn't know where he is. He's outside and the night is too still. He swears he can hear men breathing through the cinderblock wall against his back.

He fell asleep. Goddamnit, he fell asleep without knowing his position or who's on duty. His gun? His knife? ¿Dónde 'stán? He can't find his boots or pants and he can't look for them. He can't go back through the creaking door that must have woken whoever is stepping toward him. He sweats through his white undershirt and boxers. They'll find him.

He inhales. He needs a breath, a breath to orient himself. Then he can move.

Perimeter: Skinny trees. Gun nests? Negative.

Beyond: Darkness. No mortars. No moon.

Twelve o'clock: Shed. Sleeping dog. No movement, no light.

Two o'clock: Chicken coop. No movement.

Six o'clock: Structure. Small. Cinderblock. Headquarters? A camp? Krauts inside.

Eight o'clock: Movement along the wall.

"Tino?"

A voice. A woman. A trick.

He presses his shoulder blades against the wall, waiting, waiting for the voice to come closer. He inches toward the edge of the wall, creating no sound with his footsteps, holding his breath. It calls his name again. It rounds the corner. He lunges, leading with his right arm, his strong arm, hooking it around the shadow's neck, pressing his forearm into the Kraut's windpipe.

Choke or stab? He hesitates. The knife in his free hand feels too big. The man in his arm, pressed against his chest, the man hardly breathing, feels too small.

He hears his name again in a voice he knows, a voice steady like the Ave Marías he prays each night at his altar.

"Tino. It's me," the voice says, swallowing. "It's me."

The body he's holding shudders.

"Soy yo, Tino."

He exhales, dropping the knife.

Right before he blacks out, his young wife turns to face him. She stands before him like a ghost in her white nightgown, looking lost and afraid in this place that must be their home.

Before she was my mother

She soaked a washcloth in a cup of warm manzanilla and brought it to her lip, traced the jagged edge of her tooth with her tongue. She felt her lip a pomegranate, her tooth in seeds.

The next morning, she woke to her father's tears. Pressing her against his chest, his shoulders heaving, he cried, "I'm sorry, mija. Oh gosh, your daddy is sorry."

She missed two days of school. My grandpa never hit her again.

My mom tells me about my Great Grandma Jesus, who everyone called Susi, who raised seven children by herself and always looked like an old woman, even though she was only fifty-eight when she died

Men loved her.

**The night Grandma dies and my mom and I drive
back to Deming from the hospital, she tells me how
lucky my grandma was compared to her sisters to be
with a man like Grandpa**

He didn't hit her.
He didn't drink.
He wasn't a cheater.

My dad never drank at home

I remember the night shadows broke the strip of hall light under my bedroom door, my mom asking, "Where have you been?"

I snuck out of bed, turned my door handle, opening in time to see him shove her past our school pictures in their wooden frames. Her dark blue housecoat disappeared into their bedroom. He turned, grabbed his belt buckle and growled, "Go back to bed!" My brothers and I sank into our dark rooms. I think my mom cried, "I'll never forgive you for this."

Other nights before bed my dad would fluff my pillows, secure door and window locks, check the oven and stove burners, lower the thermostat to sixty, calming each room as he switched off lights.

With him out so late, who had dead-bolted the back door? Who had turned the oven knob to zero?

I sat up the rest of the night, wooden headboard against my back. Light from the hall kept me awake.

The Headlight

I was nine years old when I failed the eye test at school. Even though my mom and three older brothers all wore glasses, I felt a strange kind of shame that my eyes couldn't perform, that a part of my body was somehow less than. The day I got my glasses—ugly, boxy things with a little square on the bridge of my nose—I stepped out of the house to our backyard. The edges of the mulberry leaves jumped at me. I had never seen them before that day, ridged and jagged like the fingernails I would bite off those nights when my baby brother would cry and cry, and my mom would load us into the Oldsmobile and drive through Deming's dark and empty streets to get him to fall asleep.

Sitting next to him, my hand on his car seat, I felt useful, needed. My three older brothers were already out of the house, away at college. Some nights I would walk to my mom's bed, and she'd let me stay. I think my being there helped her too.

It's dark, past my bedtime. My dad has already moved out. My mom made arrangements for me to visit my uncle and his family the week my dad left our house. My aunt keeps a messy house. She tells her kids they'll get worms if they eat too much sugar, but she doesn't take the sugar away. We go to Western Playland, and my cousin makes me ride the Mouse Trap, a rickety roller coaster that feels like it's going to run off the rails onto the summer asphalt.

I don't know how a dad moves out of a house. What does he take with him? Blue truck. Boot cut jeans he wears with sneakers or work shoes, but never with boots. Wallet. Shoe shine box he made from scrap wood. The white underwear and undershirts and black socks from his side of the dresser, but he leaves the change in his top drawer, and I want to say he left it for me, so I can keep filling the penny and quarter rolls we'd fill together and take to the bank for new bills. What does a dad take when he moves out? Not kids. He's not the one who does things for us. He doesn't soak the beans or wash the dishes. He doesn't set the table or wipe down the counters and stove after dinner. He doesn't go to the grocery store. When I have a sore throat, he makes me hot lemonade with honey. He takes the sleeping bags and camp stove and lantern and tent out of the garage bin when we go camping and puts it all away when we come home. When he catches fish, he lifts out the bones with a fork, then dips the fish halves in egg and bread crumbs and makes homemade tartar sauce. What does he take when he leaves? Not the comal, not the coffee table or can opener or the black and white chair with the cow pattern. Maybe he takes a set of sheets, the green suitcase with a hard shell, shaving foam, and a crossword puzzle book.

My dad stays in the extra bedroom at Grandma Rosie's house. Soon he'll get a one-room apartment above Emilio's barbershop with green walls like the bottom of a swimming pool even though it's on the second floor. He'll say I can visit whenever I want and maybe we can have dinner once a week. I'll spend one night on Grandma Rosie's couch and visit the apartment once. The apartment is one big room. There's a bed with a metal headboard against the wall. There's an electric stove in the kitchen corner and a round table and two chairs for eating or reading Reader's Digest or doodling or all the things he'll have more time to do now. Where would I sit? What would we do together?

I want to ask my dad, Why do you live here?

Sometimes at night we drive past Grandma Rosie's house, and even though my mom doesn't say it, I know we're looking for my dad's truck in the driveway, and since Grandma doesn't drive, there shouldn't be any other vehicles. One night we pull into the parking lot of the Stagecoach Motel. My dad's truck is there. He steps outside into our headlight beam. A woman with big black hair and round glasses fills the doorway behind him. She's not the woman I know about, my friend's mom who works for a dentist and is married to the meat manager at Safeway and who blessed my forehead when I had a sleepover with her daughter, someone I've known since second grade. We're in the same Girl Scout troop, the one that sold the most cookies in Deming last year.

"Daddy!" I call, opening my door.

"Stay in the car, Michelle!" my mom yells. She's charging toward my dad. She left her door wide open. The car is still running. I think of the gas we're wasting, how you shouldn't leave a car running in a garage because that's how people die—but what about outside? I don't know how long we'll be here, if I should turn the key and shut the engine. But what if I do it wrong, and the engine goes off, but the battery stays on, and then we can't leave when we want? I stay where I'm told, next to my little brother. I hold onto the door handle. I have one foot on the floorboard. The other dangles above the driveway gravel. I don't want to get my slippers dirty.

Red and green horses charge toward us in neon, never advancing beyond the sign flashing "Affordable • Clean Room • -acancy."

I expect my dad to come with us. This must be the reason we came. He glances my direction, but he doesn't say hi. He doesn't wave or open his arms. He doesn't smile. He's not the dad I know, the one who crouches down at the end of the hall and calls, *véngase, véngase, véngase,* while I run to him and knock him over. Not the dad who gets up early on Saturday mornings to watch Bugs Bunny cartoons with me. Not the dad who pats the couch cushion next to him and says, *Let's have one of our daddy/daughter talks.* This dad stands in front of the big hair woman. He's a suit of armor, a shield protecting her from my mom, from us. I can't see everything. Or I don't. A fist. A shove. A handful of hair in my mom's grip. My dad's hands on my mom's shoulders. I can't make out what they're saying. A shout. A scream. A cry.

When my mom gets back in the car, she is angry-quiet. I don't ask what happened or who was with my dad. In memory we drive back home through haze. We turn to dust in our driveway and wake the next morning in our bodies, in our beds, like nothing happened.

*

My dad says I can visit any time, even spend the night if I want. But I don't really want to. I like my room at home with my pink walls and purple carpet. I like riding bikes with my friends. I don't have a bike or friends at Grandma's house, and there's not a bedroom for me, so I have to sleep on the couch in the living room under the velvet Jesus with his bloody hands. And then when my dad drops me off or my mom picks me up, she always approaches my dad. She faces him, he turns to the side, his head down. Her lips move. His don't. She talks with her hands. Maybe his shoulders shrug. But no words. My mom likes words, and she sighs and spits them into the steering wheel on the way home or into the clean towels she's folding as my dad drives back to Grandma and velvet Jesus or the swimming pool apartment. My mom might interrupt herself to ask me about the visit. *Did your Grandma say anything? Did anyone go by the house? Did your dad get any calls?*

I always say no, and I think this is true.

*

Before he moved out, my dad and mom would yell at each other behind the heavy wooden door separating the garage from the kitchen. I picture my mom throwing things at the wall and floor—Reader's Digest Condensed Books, a box of Tide, its powder scattered across the floor like salt—hurling something, anything out of him. My dad is stone, until he isn't. He might kick the laundry basket or the side yard door or the heat letter press machine he used to make magnetic signs he'd sell to businesses for their work vehicles. He was always trying to find a way to work for himself, to be his own boss, to not be poor. This is something he gave to me. That drive, that need to create my own path, to choose my own work. I remember the nice, old white couple who sold him the equipment, how the man did a demonstration in our garage. I wonder how much my dad paid for everything, if he ever made the money back, when he finally gave it up.

They were behind the door one afternoon when I got home from school. My mom was home earlier than normal. My brother's diaper bag was on the kitchen floor, dropped there like something forgotten. His bottle lay on the counter, runny formula in a shallow pool around the nipple, a circle of sugar ants closing in on the milk. My brother must have been in his crib or his car seat. Sometimes he lay on his stomach on a baby blanket in the living room. I was trying to get him to roll over, but he hadn't picked it up yet.

"I don't put sugar in the formula," my mom said from behind the garage door. "Who made it?"

I didn't hear what my dad said, but I knew he was lying—about what he did when he should be working or looking for a job, about how he knew which apartment belonged to my friend when he dropped me at her place for a sleepover, about the sugar in the bottle.

I didn't want them to catch me listening. It wasn't their fighting that embarrassed me, but my want. I wanted to hear the words they hurled at each other. I wanted my nose in their business, which was kind of my business, but also not, and putting my nose in their business made me metiche, entremetida, no better than the gossips my mom and grandma complained about at Grandma's kitchen table.

I stared at the bottle, the liquid so clear I could almost see through it. Who puts sugar in a baby bottle? I thought. Who mixes in so much water that there's hardly any milk? Somebody stupid. Somebody who doesn't know anything about kids. Somebody who doesn't care if she ruins my brother's teeth or makes my parents fight.

Quiet. From behind the door, my mom called in her phone voice, "Michelle, go to your room, okay?"

I pictured the muscles in her neck, her jaw tight, her stunted inhale and exhale shuddering her shoulders.

*

The woman from that night went to our church and always sat in one of the front pews with her adult daughter at the eleven o'clock Mass. I don't know if she was married.

*

My older brother caught them on 8th Street where he was driving back to class, like all the other high schoolers who left campus at lunch for McDonald's and Sonic, when he saw our brown Oldsmobile. Two heads. A thought: why isn't Mom at work? But it's not Mom, the hair longer, fuller. The car approaching, faster. A movement: the driver's hand waving toward the passenger. The passenger ducking down toward the floorboards.

*

Chaparral Elementary School, 4th grade. I am the second tallest girl in my class, behind the girl whose family runs the Sonic and whose jacket smells like French fries. I play volleyball. I'm well-known, which is different from being popular. I wear glasses. I want to wear knickers, striped socks, and Hush Puppies like the popular girls, but my mom says they'll be out of style by next month so why spend the money? Dini is a sixth-grader. She moved to a house around the corner from ours over the summer. While they were building it, my friend Yvette and I would ride our bikes through the rooms without walls and imagine where our bedrooms would be. Yvette is in fifth-grade. She lives next door to Dini and across the alley from me. Sometimes Dini is my friend, and sometimes she is Yvette's friend. When she is my friend, we make fun of the old cars in Yvette's yard and of her dad who walks with a wooden leg and talks in a high voice. When she is Yvette's friend, Yvette calls me and tries to get me to say mean things about Dini, and even though I want to (like how I know she took my only Barbie and made up the story about her grandma making a dress for it so I wouldn't tell on her), I don't because I can hear Dini's brothers watching Nickelodeon in the background, and I know Yvette doesn't have cable so she's calling from Dini's house, and if she's calling from Dini's house, then Dini is listening from the phone in her parents' bedroom while Yvette talks from the phone in the kitchen.

Dini's hair feathers perfectly, and her mom buys her whatever clothes she wants. I'm playing hopscotch with Cathy and Adina near the fourth-grade classroom doors and the water fountain that bubbles up from a concrete square. I'm about to get a drink of water when I see Dini and her tall sixth-grade friends walking toward me. I stand up taller because she must want to be my friend now, and she's going to be my friend in front of her other friends. I take another drink of water so I don't look like a loser waiting for her to talk to me. I think she's going to say hi or invite me to her house or a party, but instead she says, "Your parents are getting a divorce."

"I know," I say, even though I don't, even though no one in my family has told me. But really, I do. I know by the burn that starts in my stomach and reaches down between my legs so I have to pee, and I don't want to, not here, not in front of her and all her stupid friends, like the one time at volleyball practice when Coach wouldn't let me go to the bathroom and sometimes at night when I dream I'm walking a dock above a lake or river but the dock is full of holes and if I'm not careful I'll fall and I always fall and when I wake up, my sheets and nightgown and mattress are wet and it's too late at night and too early in the morning to wake anyone and I'm too afraid to cross the hall to the bathroom so I stuff my sheets and my panties and dirty pajamas under my bed and change underwear and try to fall back to sleep on the bare mattress.

Dini says, "Your mom called my mom crying because your dad's having an affair with M____'s mom, and he's moving out next week."

"Okay," I say, squeezing my insides all the way to my toes inside my tennis shoes and all the way up to my teeth.

She turns, and her pack turns with her.

Adina says, "She's lying."

Cathy says, "Yeah, she doesn't know."

"Yeah," I say, but I know she's right. And because she knows, I know Yvette knows, and if Yvette knows, then her big mouth mom, who goes to every funeral even for people she never met, knows. And all the yelling, and my dad knowing where M____'s apartment was, and the sugar-water baby bottle make sense. I am good at making everything okay, so I stuff Dini's words into my pencil case and zip it and put it at the way back of my desk, so a few days later when my mom tells me that she and my dad are getting a divorce I cry and cry like I am so surprised, but when I ask why, my mom says that they keep fighting and sometimes this happens and it doesn't mean they don't love each other. They still love me and my brothers, and they will always be our parents. I try every way I can to get her to tell me about M____'s mom. What happened? What do you fight about? Will you and Dad marry other people? But all she says is, "Nobody's getting married. You don't have to worry about that right now."

She eventually tells me about the affair, about M____'s mom. I think she does it because we live in a small town, and she figures I'll find out at some point, that I've heard things, and it's better to get the full story from her. You know how people talk.

*

The divorce is fast. My dad lives with us, and then he doesn't.

I remember sleeping over at Grandma Rosie's only once before he got the apartment. I don't remember dinners, Saturdays together. What do we talk about? He looks lonely and strange in his one big room apartment with the green walls, the afternoon light coming through slats in the cinder block walls. My mom gets angry with us. She tells us, *Your dad opened a door, and you all slammed it in his face.* I think she means this for real. When did I slam the door? When did he try to come in, and I didn't let him? My brother says, *She doesn't mean an actual door.*

When the papers are signed, my mom says, "People might ask about your dad and me. The notice will be in the *Headlight* tomorrow or the next day."

I pictured an article, a black and white photo of my parents hunched over a scroll, quills in their right hands, a judge in a powdered wig hovering over them. I don't ever see the notice. Nobody asks me about it.

*

My parents remarry each other eighteen months after their divorce. It starts with my dad stopping by the house for dinner on a Wednesday, then most nights of the week, then him staying after my brother and I have gone to bed. He's not there in the mornings. It's still my mom loading her teacher things into the car and packing my brother's diaper bag and dropping me off at the bus stop. She does everything. Except for one day when she sits on the floor in front of the hall closet, their wedding album in her hands, her dress spilling out of its bag, my mom is fine. She still goes to work and grades papers and does lesson plans and makes dinner and helps me with homework and takes us to church and buys our clothes and takes us to visit Grandma and Grandpa. She makes my brother's formula and bathes him and tucks him in at night. And when he can't sleep, sometimes she'll load us in the car and drive and drive until he's quiet. She doesn't really need my dad. Except maybe she does because they exchange vows in City Hall. Dad wears his only suit, light brown polyester. We don't think to make tissue paper flowers to put on the car for a procession, but as we're ironing clothes and taking showers and curling hair, my dad approaches me with a green chile in his hand and says, "We're going to put these on the car. To decorate. With streamers." My dad was creative, but he never had the means or the luxury of expressing his creativity in the world. He had jobs—John Deere, Deming Office Supply—not a career. I'd put green chile on a car today. Rasquache. Kitsch. But back then we were a brown family coming back together in a brown town that held us close to the dirt. My dad in his shiny suit. My brother in a car my grandparents had purchased new, then sold to my uncle, who later sold it to my parents, who then gave it to my brother. Why draw attention to ourselves? Why say, Hey, we're Mexicans who don't speak Spanish, and our parents are getting remarried after my dad's affairs divorced them, even though nothing's changed, except my dad's not with those women anymore? I think we had a cake from Deming Pastry. I think my Grandma Rosie was there, but my mom's parents were not. We felt a strained kind of happy. There's one picture from that day, all of us in City Hall. Dad in his suit. Mom in a below-the-knee blush-colored dress and a pin corsage. If you remember the remarriage, then you have to remember the divorce, which means you have to remember the affairs and the fighting and maybe some drinking too. Sixth-grade me knew that my mom gave in too easily, that she lost something by taking him back, knew that he needed her and us more than she needed him.

Sixth-grade me thought she knew everything.

The anger from my mom's parents lasts and lasts. My dad doesn't go with us to visit. There's not a conversation or a confrontation but a wearing down of my grandma's rage until we are together for my brother's wedding, my mom's Master's degree ceremony, Saturday dinner when the out-of-town cousins come to visit.

Sixth-grade me didn't know how much I needed him, how much I would and do. It would all be worse if he had stayed away. He wasn't the kind of dad who would take us school shopping or cook dinner for us or check our temperature when we were sick. He was roast a weenie on a gas burner with a fork dad, change the motor oil himself and bury it in a hole at the edge of the yard dad. Build me a wooden chair and paint it white dad. Get a taste for something different and try out a recipe from a magazine kind of dad. Were he and my mom still divorced that day he and I made chicken cacciatore? Neither of us knew the difference between a head and clove of garlic, and when I called my grandma to ask, she said, "Mi'ja, you don't have to cook. I'm making dinner." And I couldn't say I was with my dad because she was so angry with him. But my dad was capable. He could and would show up for me, for all of us, in powerful ways. The chicken cacciatore, the city hall wedding are the beginnings of a decades-long redemption.

*

My mom has been painting the house all day, all summer really, giving each room an accent wall in burgundy, plum, or midnight blue. The picture frames are stacked and leaning against the back door, our faces pressed into each other, frozen in smiles.

"Have you seen the world news today?" she asks, picking up *The Headlight* from the kitchen table. It's an eight-page daily that publishes every letter to the editor and the local police blotter. "Every year they do the same picture." She points to the cover photo, children splashing at the city pool. "At least it's in color now."

My eyes scroll to a headline, *Local Teen Killed in Accident*. "Did you know her? Was she ever in your class?"

"I never had her, but I know her grandma."

"Who?"

"Este, the one church," she says, scraping burgundy paint from her thumbnail. I picture the Stagecoach, the woman with black hair and round glasses.

"She's the one—"

"Yeah," she answers, looking up at me. She rolls in her lips and sighs.

"There was one night when we went to look for them, we found them. Daniel and I were with you."

"I forgot you were."

"What happened?"

"Jimmy Vasquez came to the house." Jimmy worked with my dad at the John Deere company in Deming. Side by side they looked like oversized elves in their forest green pants and shirts. "Your dad told me he wasn't with her anymore. But Jimmy came over shouting, 'Comadre, I saw them. They're at her mom's house.' So I got in the car and went to find them."

"But we were with you. Daniel and I were with you."

"Yeah. I guess you were. I drove to the house—"

"Not a hotel?"

"No mi'ja, it was a house. It was her mom's house."

"Are you sure? I always pictured a neon sign."

"It was a house. Your dad's truck was there. They were standing outside. When he saw me, your dad started yelling to her, 'There she is. Get in the car. Get in the car.' Híjole. I was so angry. I got down from the car. I don't even know what I said."

"Did you hit her?"

My mom's eyes widen. She takes in a sharp breath like something startled her—a black widow or a roach running across her bare feet. Her mouth is open. But then she closes her lips and the corners of her mouth go up like she remembered a secret.

"I guess I did," she says, peering past the kitchen and living room out the screen door, across the cul-de-sac and beyond the field of mesquite bushes. She covers her mouth, her thumb resting on her jaw, and talks through her fingers, braced over her open mouth like bars. "Ay. Dios mío. I guess I did."

It's midday. The sun is directly over the house. Its rays sharpen the details, make the edges of the doorway leading outside and the bushes in the yard crisp, clean, focused.

In my mind I am a little girl again. This time I am riding shotgun. The neon horses are charging. They lift off the sign and barrel through the parking lot into the burgundy night. And when the dust settles behind them, everything is quiet, still. The lady with the big hair and glasses is gone. We leave the motel. Mom, Daniel and me in the Oldsmobile. Dad, still part of us, following in his truck, our headlights on, moving silently through the streets of Deming like a funeral procession. Maybe we start again, this time with no yelling, no crying, no guilt or shame. Daniel falls asleep. We drive and drive. My dad follows, and through the dust, the night, past the charging horses, we find our way home.

North / Mictlampa | 129

Herencia
abuelo materno—Florentino

He thought it would be prettier. France.

He'd imagined it green, unlike Dolores and the ranch where he was raised. The animals fuller, the people softer. He'd imagined rolling hills, wildflowers, and sweet scents—alhucema, ruda. He'd imagined a place where corn, lettuce, and onions grew without brown men bending over them, without buckets of water pulled up from the well he'd dug with his father and uncles. He'd imagined water without sediment, villages owned by no one, fathers with unstained hands, mountains with no mineshafts, air and soil without a layer or even a hint of coal dust.

But how could he even see France? It was more a place he sensed, crawling across it, not like a baby on hands and knees, but on forearms and belly, elbows tucked close as he crept under barbed wire, scanning trees for gun nests. Or perhaps he knew France more intimately than her own people, closer to her than he'd been to his wife in months.

At first, the mortar lights recalled the Texas lightning storms he'd watched from the fence post where he tethered his donkey each night as a boy.

There were donkeys in France. One he could have toppled by tapping with his bayonet, its belly bloated, its bray hardly audible, like a dog with no bark. He had nothing to give it. Only the cigarettes in his C-rations and a box of wet matches. He could have gutted it with his bayonet, the donkey's blood not even gushing. A slow drip. He could have eaten it raw.

He thought it would be prettier.

Secrets leak. Words never uttered pass in the seed from man to woman, in the milk from mother to child.

His disappointment, his fear, they drip down through his children, grandchildren, generations he could never imagine. They drip down to me. The unpaid debts. The ones who got away. A lot of good men filled that ship that crossed the Atlantic to Europe. He returned.

Each time he kisses my forehead, holds my hand for grace, he passes on our herencia—coal dust, a donkey's echoing bray, a German boy's last words, and the final cries of all those good men whose spirits floated back across the sea as their blood soaked the French soil.

Love Story
Bad Boyfriend

Him: I think about you, Michelle. I do. That day you called to say you wouldn't be in class I took down your number. I was going to call you when the semester ended. I think about you. And I don't just think about getting laid—I mean, I think about that too. But I think about what it would be like to be with you.

Him: If things don't work out, we can't write about each other.

Him: This is why I didn't want to date you.

Him: You really are a classic beauty.

Him: You'll cheat on me. You need too much. Someone will give you some attention, and you'll leave me.

Him: It's not like I fucked her, Michelle.

Him: I'm trying to love you I'm   having a hard time being intimate with you, yeah you   have gained some weight   sometimes you're beautiful and sometimes   you're homely you're a big woman why don't you   trim your pussy just a little bit so it's not so hairy   your acne is really flaring up   I feel   so small next to you like a boy

Him: You must feel such peace when I'm not around.

Him: Remember when we fell asleep in the courtyard in Chartres? It was a warm day. School kids ran through the labyrinth, laughing and shouting.

I tried to get up to sketch or write, but your legs were pinning mine. I couldn't move. At first I panicked.

But then the sun was on your face. A woman in the rectory smiled at us through white lace curtains. And instead of feeling trapped, I felt rooted. By you.

Him: Let me tell you what I like about us. No matter how hard it gets we try to make it work.

Him: I feel all this pressure to fall in love with you. When I look at you I want to love you. But I don't.

Her: Well. There it is.

distress

acute physical or mental suffering; affliction; trouble

distress

a state of extreme necessity or misfortune

Ritual

Cihuateteo extend their longest fingers of orange and red to our side of the mountain at sunset, when we remember dry heat is not a myth, that dusk and darkness bring relief. The cinder block wall softens, as spirits enter the backyard of the El Paso house where I've rented a room since coming back to El Paso a few months ago.

It is early spring, and soon the winds will come, but tonight the air is still. I kneel on a concrete slab next to Bad Boyfriend's fictions, print outs of the emails we exchanged while he was in Europe, and his gift of Neruda's *Veinte Poemas de Amor y Una Canción Desesperada*. A box of matches and a heavy rock hold everything in place. I ask the spirits to lend their breath to the fire as I light a match and hold it to crumpled pages of his manuscript.

When we broke up, and I ran from El Paso to my parents' home in southern New Mexico, I packed his words in a box with *Pedro Páramo*, *Artemio Cruz*, and my journals. Months later I brought the box to this house and unpacked its contents onto a shelf with other Latino writers, but his writings didn't fit. His manuscript hung over the edge. His short story collection was too tall to stand upright and too wide to lie flat under *Loose Woman*, *Mother Tongue*, *So Far From God*. At night I imagined his book complaining to me about the attention I denied it, his manuscript demanding a prominent spot on my bedside table. He once said I was good at putting myself first, that his work didn't matter enough to me.

I rip the cover from his collection and twist it into kindling. Next the title page with his signature and dedication, *Hope you like this book as much as I like you.*

The mountain holds us in the folds of her skirt, shielding us from west-side winds and Juárez lights. I brush my hair from my face with my fingers and nod toward the ghosts gathered along the backyard wall that stands high enough to block our neighbors. Women running. Women walking barefoot. Women with dusty trensas, gourds balanced on their heads, babies in rebozos on their backs. Women with ferocious eyes.

Women dipped in water, the Río Grande dripping down their backs like a blessing. Winged tongues flying over their heads to my ears, offering prayers, wishes, instructions. I believe these winged tongues can lift me.

I add one page at a time to the fire.

"I won't read his books," I whisper. I have carried his words under my skin for centuries. His voice was the desert line where sky meets the earth, where clear and endless blue finds its roots in the packed soil that stores water and life and awaits summer monsoons.

He was Cortés.

The slab blackens. I want this stain to stay and the earth below it to remember me.

Before tonight I feared the ghosts, feared they would encircle me and choke the flames. The ghosts, my grandmothers, might say I was lucky to be with a man who never hit me, a professor with soft hands. A man who was often sober, who hardly touched me.

But tonight Grandma China rests on a lawn chair by the clothesline, an ankle crossed over the opposite thigh. Her sister sits beside her, the lines on her face smooth and soft, the roughness refined by spring winds and July monsoons. They are not afraid. They hold hands. They tell stories. They laugh. Bisabuela Jesús walks barefoot through cilantro and rosemary, a marigold in her hair. Bisabuela Eleuteria returns to us, not as Cihuateteo with eagle claws for hands and feet, like other women who die in childbirth, but restored, a young woman in a cotton housedress with kind, curious eyes. She faces the setting sun.

I burn his words and slowly return to me, seeing my reflection in the gray smoke of Tezcatlipoca, Smoking Mirror, Underworld God, Lord of the Night, of night wind, of war and crossroads. He speaks through our reflection.

When Bad Boyfriend and I broke up, he said, "I have a feeling things aren't over between us."

Tomorrow he will call to invite me to meet for coffee, to talk, to ask if we can be friends. It's as though he feels me on this side of the mountain, as though he lifts his head and smells the smoke, reads his words in it. He must know. Something in him must feel my release.

For Muertos I will drape papel picado around my bed, light candles on the floor. I will create a sugar skull of my face and then dissolve it like

Mexican chocolate in hot water. In winter I will ask los reyes for mercy. I'll bite the baby Jesus baked into the rosca and laugh because it promises a better year—one with enough to give.

South / Huitzlampa

rumbo del niño interior, de la niñez
rumbo de la voluntad

And the World Tasted of Dust
Summer 2001, La Frontera—before

My mom and I had finished loading the last of my things onto my brother's truck. I drove, relieved to have my hands on the steering wheel, out of her reach. She liked to be useful, and as long as I could remember, even when her papers were graded, the laundry folded and put away, rugs vacuumed, beans simmering and yellow cheese grated for dinner, she would rearrange the living room furniture or organize the cabinet of old margarine and cottage cheese containers we called Tupperware. Now that the truck was loaded and we were less than an hour from El Paso, she might try to hold my hand and tell me she hoped this move would be good for me or ask if I was still seeing "that counselor."

My counselor, a mexicana, specialized in trauma. A mentor who believed all Chicanos should go to therapy sent me to her. He had called after a car accident that shouldn't have shut me down but did, and I'd left Albuquerque without warning and driven to my parents' house to stay for a week. "You come from the Aztecs," he said. "Your people are warriors." Then he gave me Virginia's number. Thanks to her, I could drive again. She guided me through the telling and retelling of the accident and all the wreckage it unearthed, each time focusing on a different aspect, each time releasing a little more of my fear.

I didn't like being the center of my mom's attention or the object of her worry. Nothing she said or did could put me on solid ground. Each morning I woke in a deep hole, and by the time I clawed my way out of it, the sun had set and all that needed to be done for the day had been done by everyone else. I couldn't see a place for me. I was so tired. I felt like a disappointment. I was trying to be well, hoping the worst of me had stayed behind with the car accident, a breakup, a giving up. The breakup was a long, slow death. And once it was finally over, I spent nights with my long-time crush who always seemed to have a girlfriend in some other town but said his time in Albuquerque was all mine. And it was. He was tender, tracing a pinky across my cheek, smoothing a stray hair back from my face. He'd make us chorizo y huevo for breakfast, kiss my cheek as he left his apartment for work or class. We'd kiss for hours. He'd drive me to and from therapy while my car was in the shop. He took me to his cousin's wedding. The sweetness lasted through the summer, until this drive to El Paso. I fantasized he and I would return to each other once I was well, once there was no girlfriend, once we'd both learned whatever we were supposed to learn about life and commitment.

There were other forces that summer and fall. A stranger grabbed me while I jogged on a ditch path. That morning, like most mornings, I had run my roommate's dog. A branch snapped or maybe instinct made me turn around. He was jogging, not like an athlete but almost like a cartoon character taking big steps on his tiptoes. He wore jeans. "Hi," I shouted, looking him in the eyes. He walked around me and then cantered down the trail. I pretended to calm the dog, a lab/pit bull mix who wagged her tail as the man passed us. He jogged about fifty yards ahead of me, then turned around. I didn't want him behind me. He came closer. I waited for him to pass. It was a Monday morning. He lunged at me. He clasped the back of my left thigh and jerked his hand up to my butt. I screamed at him, felt myself taller than I really was, rage rising out of me. My scream stunned him momentarily. A breath. He didn't have a weapon. I think he meant to catch me off guard. I dropped the leash. The dog leapt toward him. He ran.

My crush was the honey in a summer of diagnoses, disorders: depression, anxiety, PTSD, a psychiatrist who wanted to prescribe pills.

*

"Are you thirsty?" my mom asked as we turned onto the farm road leading to the old highway, which would lead us back to the interstate.

"Yeah," I said, glancing at the half-dozen plastic water bottles we'd emptied since leaving Albuquerque almost three hours earlier.

I guided our conversation away from the accident and from Victor, the ex-boyfriend who I'd thought I loved and assumed would always love me. We'd been together over a year, the longest I'd been with any man since my first love. Victor was a divorced Chicano attorney with two small boys. At twenty-eight I was too young to be dating a forty-year-old with children. We met salsa dancing, and I remember thinking that night as he led me through a basic salsa step then twirled me under one arm and around his back, over and over no matter the song, always a quarter-beat off the rhythm, this is what my life might be with him. Predictable. Safe. Not quite right, but maybe right enough. We broke up because I was moving away. Or maybe I was moving so we could break up.

"Let's stop," Mom said, pointing ahead to the general store on the crossroad connecting Highway 185 to the interstate. I pulled into the parking lot, hard-packed gravel under the tires. A white tarp sign promised cold water. My mom and I got out of the truck. Since the accident, the sun hurt my eyes. I rubbed my fingers together, feeling an almost undetectable grit between them. As I blinked and swallowed, I realized the grit was in my eyes, on my teeth, coating my face and hair. I thought of the ceremonies that must have welcomed our girls into puberty, scars carved on the breast and hip, girls baptized with corn pollen by their elders, ceremonies lost or moved to shadows, lost to those of us cut off from our indigenous sides and left to claim Spain and America, cross and country. I thought of how the dust still holds those ceremonies, how our people still need them—ways to bring girls into womanhood, to welcome home the warrior, to heal the sick.

"I need to re-arrange a few things," I said, gesturing toward the truck bed.

"You want a snack or something besides water?" she asked.

"No, just water," I said, testing the strength of the bungee cord holding my mattress.

I had spent the months since the accident extracting possessions from my Albuquerque apartment and then from my friend's extra bedroom and moving south in fragments. First there had been a pressboard bookcase with removable shelves and two cardboard boxes filled with old journals. Then the mattress and box spring, raspberry stained from the insides of beetles that swarmed my brother's truck as he drove my bed south. He told me of gusts slamming the beetles against the grill and windshield, yanking the mattress from the truck bed and hurling it across the interstate. He couldn't pry it from the mesquites lining the shoulder without ripping holes in the pillow top.

I had stored everything in a friend's trailer in Leasburg, when I thought I might start over by living with him. But then I dropped off

South / Huitzlampa | 143

the last load, propped the mattress against the flimsy wall of his spare room. I looked out the window to the half-acre of land he loved, not because it was beautiful, but because it belonged to him. I think I felt the same way about him, a kind of love born from comfort, familiarity and faith that someone or something would always be there for me.

I pictured brown outs erasing the trailer. I imagined cars breaking down on the interstate, and strange men walking to our door for help. Out the window lay fine sand, a reminder of our thirst, and where the water should be, mesquite bushes and then the highway. I couldn't live there. I pictured myself alone in the trailer, behind a front door easy to kick in. Isolated, too tired to drive into town. I couldn't live there. So my mom and I drove to his place to get my things and move them to my brother and sister-in-law's new house in El Paso.

*

I tugged on the elastic cords holding my night table and box spring in place, opened and closed the duffel bag stuffed with winter clothes. I reinforced a box of breakables marked "Michelle" and "Fragile."

Much later, I would think of omens I might have heeded: the beetles, the crosswinds, the scar that today would brand on me. But here and now I believed the invitation to live with my brother and sister-in-law was a lifeline. Refuge awaited, a solid house made of brick, older brother to shelter me.

Heat rose in waves from the divided highway in front of the store, blurring rows of alfalfa and cotton on the valley floor. Ahead lay the interstate that brought me here and would always bring me back to the desert, the border.

Although a season had passed, memory of the accident lingered. A black Jetta cut across my lane, sharp left from center. We hit. Broke. I veered toward a corner lamp post. A house behind it. A concrete barricade to stop my car from hitting them both. I must have slammed the brake to the floor. I stopped short of the barricade. I think I hit my head. My chest throbbed where the seatbelt held me. I thought of bruises forming a beauty queen sash.

Two in the morning, I was alone.

"Are you drunk?" the other driver yelled, his face in my window. He was handsome, a guy I might have met shooting pool at Anodyne earlier that night. Tall and thin, smooth skin, pianist fingers.

I shook my head. "I'm calling 9-1-1," I said.

"You don't have to do that. I'm a cop."

A light in the house turned on, then off again. I stepped out of the car and walked around my busted fender, bits of shattered headlight on the street. Orange construction lights flashed on top of their barrels. There were people with him, shadows in his car. I waited for him to say he was sorry, to ask how I was.

"I can't believe you hit me," I said, staring at the metal that had been my passenger fender.

"No. You hit me," he said.

I wanted to say it was his fault. He turned from the wrong lane. He turned left in front of me when he should have gone straight. But the words didn't come. My phone was still in my hand. Police were on their way. I sat on the curb. I think he sat next to me. He would not shut up. *Didn't you see me? You were going really fast.* I never went fast on Coal. The lights were timed at thirty, and if you went the speed limit, you got green all the way up the hill and under the interstate, past Roosevelt Park and the community college to the turnoff where I rented a room in my friends' house.

A small truck stopped in front of us. The driver asked if we were okay. Jetta smiled and waved him off.

"Do you want me to wait with you?" the driver asked. I think he was talking to me, but maybe he spoke to both of us. We were an us now, a unit, a couple of twenty-somethings on a sidewalk, our cars in two heaps on a one-way street.

"It's okay," I heard myself say. "We're fine."

He left.

The officer came. Jetta stood up. "Thank you for coming, officer," he said, shaking the cop's hand. "This has never happened to me before. I don't really know what to do here." I waited for the officer to recognize him, waited for Jetta to show the cop a badge, for some familiar exchange between them. Nothing. The officer wrote on his clipboard. I cried when it came my turn to speak. "We'll get this figured out," Jetta said, his hand on my shoulder. "Don't worry. Everything will be fine."

*

I must have hit my head. The neurologist said my brain crashed into my skull. "You have a mild traumatic brain injury. But really, it's nice to see such a healthy young woman in this office." He said that some people must learn to walk again. Some lose their ability to sing. Others forget their past or how to speak. I could talk; I just didn't know what to say.

The psychiatrist I saw in the weeks following the accident was a white woman who wanted to fix me with "something in the Prozac family." I sat with her only once, the light blue fabric of her sundress parting over her knee, opening into the folds of her motherly thighs. I called her weeks later, when my auto insurance requested her assessment. She sighed when I told her I hadn't filled the prescription. "You would be functional by now," she said.

I wanted more than functional. I wanted my soul healed. I wanted to be well, happy, perhaps even blissful. I needed a curandera, the Blessed Mother, Jesus, and a priest. I needed someone barefoot to rub an egg over me and crack it into a glass of water, to blow tobacco smoke into my face, and cleanse me with rosemary and an eagle feather.

I looked east to the interstate and southeast to the Organ Mountains, their peaks, depending on the angle and the sun's place in the sky, like uncut lapis or broken bones.

My mom brought out two bottles of Deming water, the kind that flowed from our tap when I was a girl before the city began bottling and selling what was ours and chlorinating what ran from our faucets. She wore a loose white T-shirt with Raggedy Ann & Andy reading a book, boxy blue petal pushers and tennis shoes she kept white by throwing them in the washer every couple of months. Her hair had been the same, loose curls cut close to her neck and behind her ears, since I was in high school. She was adjusting to bifocals, lifting the lenses to the bridge of her nose when she had to read something up close. The scratch proof coating on her lenses looked like oil pooling on a puddle, like rainbows over her eyes when the light hit.

*

I held the bottle against my forehead and looked toward the Robledo

Mountains. From here, their blue could mean water, a lake. But closer, the blue gave way to sage and creosote, to every shade of brown, all the colors of our people in the hardened mud flaking along the edges of a puddle, the stones smoothed by wind erosion, the scree turning over itself with each rainstorm gushing water down the mountain's channels.

I tossed the bottle into the truck cab for later. My palm glistened with condensation. My mattress had shifted in the truck bed, and the red and black bungee cord strained, exposing its inner white fibers. I pictured red and black threads unraveling, white threads popping loose. I pictured the bungee coils and hook straightening against the pressure, turning loose from the truck mount and whipping in the wind like a striking cobra. I pictured my mattress airborne, landing against an unsuspecting windshield. A crash. My fault.

I pressed my body against the truck for leverage, the top of my head against the propped up mattress, my face directly over the truck bed. I gripped the coils of the bungee cord and unhooked it.

The hook slipped and struck my face. I jerked my head back in pain.

"Your eye! Your eye!" my mom screamed. She was standing in front of me now, pulling my hand from my face. I thought she could see something I couldn't, my eyeball dangling from its socket between my fingers or rolling in the dirt at our feet. "I need to see if it's okay." She looked over her bifocals. I couldn't see what she saw. My brow throbbed. I blinked to keep blood from dripping into my eye. "It missed your eye," she said, brushing my hair from my face. "Oh, gracias a Dios." She put her water bottle against my brow and sat me in the truck. "I'll get you some ice," she said, squeezing my shoulder. She ran back into the store.

The white label of the water bottle was now the red of watercolors. I pulled down the visor. My brow bled where the coil had opened a gash, not wide enough for stitches, but too big for a bandage. The hook had stamped a fissure next to my left eye. I thought of the tiniest of streambeds in drought, the water pooling, then dissipating, the moisture stored deep beneath the surface.

*

There are moments I wish I could freeze.

The moment before I unhooked the elastic cord. The exhalation when my car stopped short of the concrete barrier and the empty street held me, before the other driver's face filled my open window in rage, before he yelled, "Are you drunk?" so angry and sure of himself, I almost believed I was drunk, that I had somehow caused him to make an illegal turn in front of me. The moment on the trail when instinct told me to run. But instead I froze because no one would bother me while I walked a pit bull. That man grabbed me anyway. He groped my thigh. He took off when I let the dog loose. He laughed. He looked over his shoulder and laughed.

There are moments yet to come.

The space between my inhale and exhale when my grandmother's heart stops beating and her spirit ascends, light into light, before her heavy absence settles over my war vet PTSD grandfather and me, and each of us carries a part of it home. Her death will open fissures in me, a river running underground, a splinter beneath the surface of the skin, there, pulsating, shaping life around it, but never seen, never talked about.

When I tell this story, I touch my face, lay fingertips on the scar in my brow and the other even I mistake for age. "It just missed my eye," I say.

I give thanks to shock, its mercy, its power to numb me from pain. I cup my hand over my eye, almost tasting blood as it pools on my palm.

Callus
after

I pick dead skin off my toes and pile it on the tan comforter of my grandma's bed. Most nights she slept here, sometimes in the back room with my grandpa, but his restless thrashing would keep her awake. She kept her underwear and nightgowns in the pine dresser I can almost touch from the bed. My grandpa says Mexican families mourn forty days and forty nights, but I think he's making that up, confusing Lent with lamentation. Maybe we are not to leave the house and re-enter life; maybe we throw in every rite and ritual we know. Drape the mirrors with black cloth, fast from sunrise to sunset, walk barefoot on sharp stones, and burn the bed sheets of the dead.

Gunfights play from Grandpa's bedroom television. These are his nights since she died a week ago. My grandpa doesn't sleep when he should. Instead it's one continuous Western, Gunsmoke, good guys fighting bad and never losing their white hats, Bonanza, Ben Cartwright widowed three times, his boys losing their loves to a faster draw or death. The rest of the family has gone back to the places they live, so my parents, who live a five minute drive past dirt lots of trailer homes and mesquite bushes, and I take turns sleeping over in this house where my mom was raised, this house that has evolved from cinder block and one bedroom to drywall and stucco, two bedrooms, extra bath and room for guests.

My mom says Grandpa is not my responsibility, but I have nowhere else to go. When I left El Paso, left Bad Boyfriend and the arroyo between his house and my apartment, and came to Deming, my grandma was well.

Grandpa leaves the house only to visit his heart doctor and the cemetery. I think he secretly fears she will return while he is out, and not finding him home, she will disappear forever.

*

We all thought he would die first. The sick one. The weak one. The consentido.

But even before the cancer, she knew he would outlast her. "Your grandpa's gonna live forever," she once told me. "That man doesn't have a care in the world."

*

Bad Boyfriend always fell asleep first, always turned to his side at the edge of the bed, a box spring and mattress on the dull wood floor, his back to me, his face toward the bedroom door he kept closed in the summer to concentrate the damp air panting down on us from the only functioning vent in his house. Dog hair, dust and dirty socks balled up between the mattress and the wall. Paco slept in a dog bed at our feet. I would lie on my back, close enough to feel the heat coming off his body, but closer to my own side of his full-sized mattress, one ankle crossed over the opposite knee, scraping violet polish, already weeks old, off my toenails, then peeling the calluses off my big toe and heels with the nails on my thumb and index finger and flicking my dead skin toward the wall. I tried to draw my breath from below my gut, from a solid place inside my body, tried to keep my hand steady so as not to wake him. But eventually the dust powdering his windowsills and floors would settle in my throat and lungs, and I would wake him with a cough that shook the bed.

*

Those last ten days in critical care, she didn't like him hovering in her room. He made her nervous, standing there reading aloud the numbers on the screens above her bed, as though he understood the intricacies of heart rate and lung saturation. She asked me to bring the bills from Grandpa's dresser drawer. On top was his altar, crowded with palm crucifixes from Lenten seasons past, santitos, his Sacred Heart Jesus figurine, Chimayó dirt in a Dixie cup, a fan of prayer cards from funerals. And still, he wasn't allowed in the bottom drawer. She never liked him touching her papers.

"Tino, you don't know how I keep things."

And he didn't. He doesn't.

Settings on the dryer, how to load a dishwasher, what time to take which pill. Furosemide for blood, Digoxin for his heart. Celebrex for pain.

He thought she would always be here. For sixty years he sat down at the kitchen table and breakfast appeared before him—a bowl of Quaker Oats, half a carton of Egg Beaters, wheat toast topped with Smart Balance buttery spread, low pulp orange juice, skim milk, and a plate of sliced banana, orange, and red apple. An Old Spice bottle emptied and another took its place. Doctor appointments, the cable bill, his new windbreaker, the button loose from his gray flannel pajamas. It all got replaced, fixed, taken care of. Maybe he said thank you. Maybe he said it every day.

I bet he never pictured his life like this, starting over at eighty, having to consider so much after a lifetime of someone caring for him.

*

One night I left Bad Boyfriend's bed to cough in the bathroom, my hand guiding me along the rough plaster in the hall. The syrup with codeine had worn off, and I still had two hours before I could take another teaspoon. My stomach ached, not from anything I'd eaten, but from contracting my muscles each time my efforts to forget the cough, to breathe deeply through my nose and bypass my throat failed. I squatted over his toilet, the insides of my knees touching the cool porcelain, and vomited. When I returned, he was awake, on his back, the bedside lamp spotlighting his smooth stomach. I loved his mestizaje, his hairless chest, his black eyes and hair, his skin more leche than café, but not white. We were of the same people and being with him could have felt like home. He called my body womanly, said being with me made him feel nervous, sometimes childlike. He showed me tenderness in class, praised my writing, asked challenging questions, observed my vulnerabilities. I loved that he was a little off, in need of care, motherless and childless.

I loved that he was ten years older, forty to my thirty, a professor with his own house, shelves of books, a dog he walked every day.

"Maybe you're allergic to Paco."

"I'm not. This happens at the apartment too." He and the cough had come into my life at the same time in early spring when El Paso winds draw curtains of dust along the border.

The first time the cough woke me I was in my bed alone. He had gone to a party where he said we couldn't be seen together, he the professor, and I the student. He told me later he ran into the girl who worked the front counter at the copy center. They got drunk on tequila shots and made out in his truck.

He had stayed at my place only once, after a trip when his house had been shut up for days and the late summer heat trapped inside was unbearable, even for him. Other nights he reasoned he couldn't leave the dog alone in the house. "He's insecure," he'd say.

I lowered to the mattress and lay my head next to his stomach, wrapped an arm around his skinny leg. I cried because I hadn't slept, because no amount of cough syrup or honey or hot lemon tea soothed my body. He patted my back more like a T-ball coach than a lover of six months.

"Don't cry, baby. It won't do any good."

"It makes me feel better," I said. But he was right. My tears never evoked his empathy. They angered him, widened the distance between us. "I wish you were stronger," he once said.

*

Grandpa hit her once. It happened during his worst time—flashbacks, medications contraindicating, dropping weight, threats of suicide, before our family, our people, had language for trauma, for what war does to a soul. He hid in a motel forty miles up State Road 26. My uncle found him crouched in a corner of the room, eating saltines and a banana. He could have thrown my grandpa over his shoulder and carried him to the car, but there was no fight. He told my grandpa he was driving him to Albuquerque to visit family, and it was only three hours later, after they passed the familiar exit to my aunt's house, that Grandpa knew he was going to the VA, the psych ward, and he would not go home for a long time.

*

My grandma didn't die covered with the Mexican blanket and floral sheets I've turned down for the night, but I think she would have liked to. At the hospital between visiting hours or on long nights when the blood pressure machine woke her every hour, she told us she thought of the foods she would eat at home. Simple things—black coffee, pinto beans and Spanish rice, a red apple with the wax she'd scrape off with a paring knife. "Look at that," she'd say. "They put that on fruit to make it shine." She must have missed the smell of frying onions, of fabric softener, and Fabuloso, the Mexican disinfectant she'd buy in bulk at Sam's Club in Las Cruces. She must have missed, without ever saying it, this bed she made every morning, stripping and changing the sheets once a week. She died in a hospital in Las Cruces sixty miles away. Her heart stopped beating on a bed where many had died, and once she was still—the room cleared, the papers signed—we had to leave her. Death takes our people in more ways than one. The body goes to strangers, and we journey home alone, her spirit trailing our taillights through desert darkness.

There was a time when our people died in their homes. The family kept the body and prayed over it for nine days. Our novena is almost over and we've recited no prayers save the rosary the night before she was cremated. Our obligations pile up like the newspapers by the front door, the un-thanked sympathy cards on her kitchen table, the medication in Grandpa's pillbox, this mound of skin. And beneath it all with the clutter cleared, the rough exterior removed, perhaps life is new again, soft to the touch, and more beautiful than we could ever imagine.

But we didn't ask for new life. Nobody does.

*

Being here—in my grandmother's bed, in Deming—feels like penance without confession. Bless me, Father, for I have sinned. I resent the sufferings of men, their incapacities—Bad Boyfriend to love, Grandpa to live. Someone will always take care of them. Who will care for us, the women?

My grandparents did not say goodbye to each other. We say she was not ready to die, but I think she knew when pneumonia turned to respiratory distress and they intubated and sedated her, she would not wake up again. And it was okay with her. Not good or bad. But okay. It was time.

*

I drink water from the glass I keep on the bedside table. It's the middle of January, but I sometimes sleep with the window open when the heater comes on and the hot air filling the room, the entire house, feels like a phantom sucking oxygen from my lungs rather than giving it.

I pick at the cuticle on my pinky toe. It comes off in granules I add to the pile on the comforter. I've been wearing the same violet polish since before I broke up with him, before Grandma was diagnosed with cancer two months ago. It looks like a bruise, or like ten tiny Rorschach tests. On one nail I see a fetus. On another, a Mexican Elder twisted like a Bonsai and wrinkled like my grandma's knees, bark hardened like the calluses she sliced and flicked off her heels and toes with a razor blade held by her thumb against the crook in her index finger. She did this in her kitchen while Grandpa read the *Deming Headlight*, in sweatpants and a T-shirt, one ankle crossed over the opposite thigh. On the place mat next to her sat a sweaty beer can, a cigarette balanced on a fake crystal ashtray, and a fresh jalapeño that shrank with her every bite.

*

Weeks from now I'll see Bad Boyfriend with his new girlfriend at a party, and he will ask about my grandma.

"She died," I'll say.

"What does your grandpa do in the house by himself?"

He asks those questions for him, his future. Not for my grandpa. Not for me. He lives alone in a house, and his next-door neighbors on either side are lonely old men, men with no wives or families. "Don't think the symbolism escapes me," he once said.

One hires a Mexican guy who comes every few days to clean the yard and buy groceries. The other could be dead, and who would know?

I thought my love could spare him the same fate. He will be spared, but not by me. Bad Boyfriends don't die alone. Women will always take care of him, of them.

*

At least he asks. Most offer condolences, clichés really. *She's in a better place. It was her time.* The day my grandma died, the Red Crescent in Iran rescued a 97-year-old woman who had been trapped for nine days in the rubble of a 6.3 earthquake. They found her in bed, surviving on food and drink her children had brought in the early morning hours before the quake that claimed thirty-thousand lives. It wasn't her time.

*

Tomorrow my grandpa will sleep through his morning medication. Paxil gets him out of bed. Xanax keeps him there.

I wonder who will manage his prescriptions, sit with him in doctor appointments, who will trim his hair and nails now that my grandma is dead.

*

I wish I hadn't loved Bad Boyfriend. I wish I didn't love him still. If I were someone else I could see through him, smell the unwashed hair on his green pillowcase, like tamarind left too long in the sun. That smell lived in his sheets, on my hands. I could read the tobacco stains on his teeth and index finger. Someday he'll die, simply run out of air like my grandma. He gave up smoking, but bums cigarettes off his students. He beats his chest with a fist when marijuana burns his lungs, says it's allergies, but adds his doctor found "the beginnings of emphysema." Then he passes the joint to me, keeps pushing it toward me even after I put up a hand and shake my head.

*

I stopped coughing after I broke up with him, after I packed up my El Paso apartment and drove to my parents' house in Deming, days before my grandma's doctor read the spot on her lungs. Positive. A plus sign. A cross. My fingernails work like a razor on the ball of my big toe. Not as sharp, but tenacious. Too much skin comes off between my fingers. I press my thumb against the pinhole of blood springing to the surface.

*

I lie alone in my grandmother's bed. A mound of dead skin on her comforter. TV gunshots muffled through the walls. My grandmother is ash, Bad Boyfriend dust, my grandfather a ghost who can no longer see his reflection. The me that was waits for what comes next, to be scattered like ash or reshaped and held together with spit and desert dirt.

Moving Pictures

In the picture, my bangs hang over my eyebrows, almost covering my eyes, but not enough to block the sun. One hand forms a loose tiny fist. The other cradles it like a protective shell, nestled in the fold of my lap between my skinny thighs. I lean on the white brick ledge beneath our living room window, not centered in the frame or the photo.

My shirt's colors run together. Yellow stripes morph into blue to red to green, as though I melted all my crayons into the fabric at once. My jeans—bell-bottoms handed down from one brother to another to the next to me—hang above my white socks, like feet dangling from a high chair.

I don't know who took the picture, but his shadow casts a wary screen over the grass and sidewalk at my feet. He is incomplete—a bent arm, a shoulder, a head. But he looms taller than a real person, as tall as all of me standing.

A spot blurs my features. I can't tell if it's filtered sunlight or time's breath on an unprotected print. But I know I am not smiling, I know my hazel eyes look somewhere beyond the lens.

My body is pressed close to the glass, and only a small part of me extends to shadow. Soon the shadows will blend and swallow me.

*

Alma placed a trashcan at my feet. She was my therapist that summer in Albuquerque. I was twenty-nine, an unemployed Harvard grad with Post-Traumatic Stress-Disorder.

My thighs anchored me to the couch where I sat for two hours each week while we dredged bodies from my river. The rest of me folded over, my chest and face inches from the empty can. Over the rim, the little girl with bangs and cupped hands looked into me from her picture on the coffee table. My insides spilled and filled the can, the room, Alma's notebook, my file—the official record of my disorder.

Alma said, "Michelle, you're safe."

Bent over the can, I turned over words: Post-traumatic Stress

Disorder, dis-order, a lack of order, dis-ease, a lack of ease, dis-pleasure, dis-comfort. Dispensable. Disposable.

I wanted something to fall, something besides tears and trapped words. I wished the block in me were like meals I could expunge with two fingers pushed to the back of my throat. I wanted a malady everyone could see—finger notches, my arm in a sling, gauze and medical tape covering something too delicate and horrible to expose. Instead my family saw the same me they knew in pictures—me clutching a spelling bee trophy, flanked by Mom and Dad; me in black cap and gown, holding a Harvard diploma; me hugging students in navy blue uniforms; me in a business suit standing over a lectern.

Alma said, "Your mind is like a river, and each trauma pollutes the river. When you retell the trauma, you take the junk out so the water can flow again. You turn full color memories to black and white, so it's like a picture you're seeing instead of a movie you keep reliving.

"You are worth the cleansing. And once we work through this, you will think clearly. You'll sleep through the night. You'll feel something other than fear."

Normalcy ahead—press on.

Behind my closed eyes, I walked along my polluted waterway, Alma's voice guiding me. My mind saw the silver links of Rebecca's collar attached to the leash she wore when we jogged. Here and now, there was no man jogging in jeans. This time, when his shoes snapped a branch behind me, I turned and made eye contact, threw him off with my assertive hello. This time, he ran in front of me and kept running off the trail, out of the neighborhood, far from memory.

But Alma and I knew better. We knew he jogged past me and then turned back. We knew he had grabbed me. I saw his hands, but they must be like my hands, his skin the same shade of brown, like cinnamon. The same slope from thumb to forefinger. His thumb and forefinger clamped on my hamstring, starting at the bottom and jerking up the muscle to my panties. He widened his fingers and pressed them into my hip. His thumb like a razor up the middle seam of my shorts. He didn't rape me. Couldn't knock me down. I screamed, can't remember what, scared him. Scared him. Chased him off the path, to the street, into the neighborhood. Gone.

We knew he was running there still.

If I'd gone home when the path emptied, worn sweats instead of running shorts, if I'd taken a cell phone like Victor, my boyfriend, said, I'd be on my own couch, normal, numb, dispassionate.

"Keep going," Alma said. "What are you remembering? What else is in your river?"

With my eyes closed, I saw the Rape Crisis Center, an unmarked building, a refurbished house in a row of houses. A neighborhood with cottonwoods, nice apartments, a laundromat.

"I see other women like me. We're sitting in a circle. And our therapist, Maya, keeps asking us questions, telling us we're safe."

"What do you see?"

"A couch with throw pillows and teddy bears. A coffee table with tissue boxes on it."

"What else?"

"A Raggedy Ann doll," I say, my memory drifting from the crisis center. "It belonged to me when I was a little girl."

I walked alone again, Alma's voice in the cottonwoods along the bosque.

"It's okay. You're safe. Hold the doll to you. Do you feel it?"

I paused, capable of only one toxic cleanup at a time. I opened my eyes and returned to Alma's can, Alma's couch, the fingerprints never found but still felt under my skin, embedded in bone.

*

I look good. I am wearing the red sequined dress I bought for the Millenium party. Victor smiles. Our heads are pressed together like conjoined twins. His hand seems to swallow mine. The other hooks around my waist and pulls me into him, as though he's afraid my smile is fake and I'll run, leaving only a sparkly red shoe. But this night I lean into him. I leave my hand in his. This night, after a forgettable meal, after dancing to rancheras and 80s music, we will make love for the first time. I will tell him I love him. He will tell me I am beautiful.

*

My fingers clasped his thick black hair, and I studied candle-glow outline of his nose, lips and tongue as they circled my breasts. The light didn't reach his eyes. I traced the stray hairs around his nipples, two wiry strands on one side, three on the other.

"Do you feel me?"

Sheets of jaundiced streetlight entered through the mini-blind slats, yellowing the red silk lining of my dress, a discarded peel on the closet floor where I dropped it when he unzipped me. I couldn't see my shoes in the room's darkness.

"Does it feel good?"

I shuddered.

He lifted his head. "Your eyes look green."

I nodded. Tears—a purification rite, silt rolling from eyes to the mattress.

He kissed my wet cheeks and drew out of me. He slid off me, and I curled myself inside him like the closed petals of a flower.

*

I slide the red dress picture from a velvety frame on my desk. My mom would want me to keep it because I look pretty, "so happy, mi'ja." I can't extract Victor without ripping me. So I release us to the hardwood floor where scraps of us seem to float on its tinted veneer, bluish through the curtained sun. Victor's torn smile, my hand, dried rose petals. Greeting cards: Valentine's Day, my birthday, thinking of you, get well. Get well. I can't say if they're flotsam or jetsam, cargo shipwrecked or jettisoned.

*

"I miss the old Michelle," Victor said, reaching across the front seat to put his hand on my leg.

I slumped against the window, watching Alma's place shrink, then disappear in the passenger side mirror. I answered Victor inside my head: I am Teflon. Your touch slides right off.

My forehead pressed against the glass, I tried counting the yellow lines, sunshine on asphalt. The windows stayed up, sealing us in the Cavalier's conditioned air.

"Michelle. Can we talk?"

The forehead smudge blurred my reflection in the window. In the clear glass above it, Victor glanced at me, then turned back to the road as the light changed.

In my head, we'd already talked: we're pretending this is the comfortable silence shared between lovers who need no words to understand each other, that I'm tired, busy, over-extended, PMS-ing. Pretending you've been robbed of nothing, and someday the shell you sleep next to will be filled with a woman you want.

"Michelle."

"What?" I poked fingerprint eyes into the forehead blot and drew a smile with my pinky.

"Stop it. Would you talk to me?"

I turned to him. Victor's jaw tightened and quivered, the skin over his knuckles pulled taut as he gripped the steering wheel harder.

"What do you want me to do?" I wanted to sound smart. He always said I was smart. And funny. I once made him laugh. "You can't say you miss the old Michelle. That's not fair." We pulled onto I-40. "She's dead. I killed her."

Orange barrels narrowed the interstate to two lanes. I couldn't pull the words through me: You think I'd be okay if I'd taken the cell phone that morning, if I'd asked you to go with me. You think you can make me better if you keep sending flowers. You think I've forgotten how to pray. You think I'd feel safe if I moved to a place where men don't hurt women.

"I'm just wondering when someone's gonna take care of me," he said.

My palm struck the window. "Why can't you take care of your own damn self?"

I turned back to the window, the face still there, unscathed. I rolled down the glass, my reflection lost in the desert sun.

*

I like this one because I look strong. This was when I coached volleyball, played guitar, and taught grade schoolers to be good Catholics. When I knew how to help others. This was before—before Albuquerque and Alma, Victor and memory.

South / Huitzlampa | 161

I flex flabby arm muscles on a pier. My pose is comic, A Chicana Miss Universe in a world very small. Ripped jean shorts, a tank top, and a smirk. Within the barrier reef, the Caribbean undulates. It's a rocking horse, a hammock—so much salt it holds you. Trust it and lie still. You can turn your back on this sea—no undertow, no waves hurling debris onto the sand. Beyond the pier's edge, beyond my muscles' reach, the clear sea deepens, reflecting the sky's greenish blue. And beyond the reef, waves froth into a jagged line separating sea from sky. I stand before it. But flip the angle, and it would saw me in half.

*

My red Cavalier rolled past the stoplight and died under I-40.

"Shit. Don't." I banged the steering wheel.

Horns honked behind me, but no one stopped. I locked my doors, imagining faces, bodies, hands reaching for me in the headlights streaking past. I scanned my cell phone. My roommates were gone, my best friend asleep.

Victor. Fuck.

He answered.

"I'm sorry. I didn't know who else to call."

He was there in ten minutes, cell phone pressed to his ear, waiting for AAA.

"Are you alright?" He hugged me, pinning my arms between his T-shirt and my tank top.

"I'm fine," I breathed into his chest.

"I'm so sorry this happened to you." He freed my arms, but enclosed my hands in his. "Why don't you sit in the car? I'll check the battery."

"I can do it." I pulled away from him. "Do you have a flashlight?"

He retrieved the toolbox from his Dodge while I fumbled for the hood release.

I scratched my thumb. "Fuck."

The flashlight beam landed on my face and inched down my bare arms. He parked the light on my hands as he approached. He lay his fingers over mine and guided them to the lever.

"Do you feel it?"

I didn't answer. I walked to his car and leaned against it, left him inspecting the battery, talking with AAA, the glow on his face changing from red to green to yellow, his lips moving, but emitting no sound I could hear over the passing cars and freeway traffic above us.

Later, after the tow truck, the silent ride home, and Victor's escort to my door, I leaned against my bed, staring into the room's familiar darkness. The candle at my feet illuminated Our Lady of Guadalupe in the cheap frame from La Basilica. There were no horns or empty engine clicks, no tow chains pulling my vehicle to its resting places, only night-stillness and an anemic voice within me begging, "Please make things easier, or send help."

*

I say the woman next to me in the photo is a college friend. Sometimes I say we met in book club or we're colleagues. I forget the stories I've invented.

We stand in a meadow in the Sangre de Cristos, mountains named for the blood of Christ. The trail beneath our feet is rocky. Wildflowers gaze at the sun as it pokes through white pelusas in the New Mexico sky. Pines and aspens seem to spring from the ruddy soil behind the meadow. They shade the trail, our way home. I clutch Rebecca's dog collar. The woman holds her leash.

I am taller, darker, longer-haired, but we wear the same eyes—unable to absorb the beauty around us.

*

We sat on the private side of unlocked doors barricaded by warnings of groups in session. Maya's voice lilted over us. She sang instructions like fold ballads, encouragement and validation like a first-grade teacher on hearing her students read.

The musty scent of donated furniture swallowed me as I sank into the armchair's southwest pastels. Tissue boxes stared at us from the coffee table in the center. I clutched a stuffed animal, the kind happy women's children place in the box of things for those less fortunate. My eyes settled behind Maya's floor pillow, her head like another title cramming the oak-like bookshelf against the wall.

At my feet, severed magazine limbs formed a jagged circle framed by

South / Huitzlampa | 163

balding tan carpet. All around me, women whose names I'm not allowed to repeat scissored and ripped through back issues of *People* and *Good Housekeeping*, preparing our survivor's show and tell.

I tore a perfect smile out of a pore-less skin, ripped flat abs from below perky breasts. I carved hips from between thighs and navel. I found a toddler in a Huggies pull-ups ad. The top of her curly head faced the camera, and she stared at her bellybutton, exploring the world inside her. Without scissors, I freed her from the page, one hand covering her tiny body, the other drawing and discarding the magazine frame. I pasted marigolds on her pull-ups, arranged loose body parts and words like woman, strong, and secret on the black poster board around her.

"Is everyone ready? Let's come back to the group," Maya said.

"Michelle, is the little girl you?"

I nodded.

"What does she feel?"

I shook my head and silently traced my finger around the flowers.

*

My family says the little girl in the photo is me—same curls her mom would trim until she could manage them on her own, same blue coat with daisy-shaped buttons. But there is a joy in her I don't recognize, something I have never seen in my own reflection.

She is still shorter than the sign that would let her on the big kid rides with her brothers. But she doesn't care. She stands next to Dad, and steps towards the camera, toward Mom, almost off the bench. Dad's hand supports her leg, so gently she doesn't even notice. She's laughing, her chin turned up and her mouth open wide enough to see all her baby teeth. One arm leans on Dad's shoulder, her palm open and facing the camera. The other lifts up and back, bending so she can touch her hair.

When the picture-taking is done, her brothers will come back from their big kid rides, and they will all go home. And for years, even after they've added another boy to the family, they will talk about this day, this picture.

But she won't remember.

My brother's heavy.

"Do you want to try something with me?"

I say uh-huh or nod my head.

I can't see his eyes behind his glasses. They're not sunglasses. They're thick, heavy on his face. And when he moves, the sun between the curtains hits the lenses so I can't see where he's looking.

The curtains are thin, like the bedspread between me and the floor. It scratches when I rub against it. No wonder he kicks it off when he sleeps. Dust floats between the opening in the curtain and his back. But it doesn't land on him, and it can't escape out the window.

"Can you feel it?"

I'm quiet, like everything else right now. My ears try to hear Dad's truck cough and spit in the driveway. If Dad came home, his truck would park next to the house, and I'd see a Chevy-shadow on Elmer's garage. Elmer's our neighbor. He collects rocks. He brings us vegetables from his garden. If Dad was home, his truck would move in front of the sun. It would fill the curtain space, and I could see the eyes above me.

"Do you feel me?"

He pushes up and presses down again.

There's space between the bottom of the closet door and the rug. It's yellow on this side, not like the sun, but like mustard in a jar. Right under the closet door it looks brown and then closet swallows it and all I see is black. If I hid on that side I'd see a crooked line of light coming from where I am now.

My eyes look for Elmer. If Elmer came, his shadow would walk over us, turn us dark then light again. His work boots would crunch small rocks under his feet, like the sound of my hand in a bag of chips. Feeding chips to Raggedy Ann. Chip bag on yellow carpet. Red Raggedy Ann head on the floor. Elmer would knock on the door and he'd have asparagus from his garden. No one would answer.

"Does it feel good?"

I want Mom's teacher shoes to clack against the stepping stones in the yard. I want the front door to swing open for her or Dad or another brother. I want her lap to hold my head, her fingers to smooth my hair until I fall asleep. She'd carry me from the living room to my bed and I wouldn't wake until morning.

My fingers try to grab the carpet yarns, but they're greasy from the

South / Huitzlampa

chips and they're small and they slip. My mouth is open so wide he must see the tooth I'll put under my pillow in a few weeks. So wide my eyes are almost closed.

"Does it? Does it feel good?"

I think it's supposed to because why would he ask. But I don't answer. I don't like to talk when I cry. I sound like a baby.

*

My eyes look up at me from the photos on Alma's coffee table. In all of them I see a woman who finally makes sense. I once told Victor I deserved to inhabit a space between worship and indifference. But I don't really believe that. In my mirror, I am stunning and hideous, visionary and myopic, brilliant and a fool. I guard my time fiercely or let it sift through a hole in my pocket. I beat me up and send me flowers the next day.

*

"It's like there are two of you," Alma said. "One is a curious, innocent little girl, and the other is this person who beats her up." She whapped a fist into her palm, a lop-sided clap punctuating each thought. "No matter what the little girl does, not matter how good she is, how smart, how kind—"

Whap.

"—the other one always knocks her down."

Through the high window over Alma's desk, the afternoon sun burned orange around her shoulders and head. Her hands jumped in and out of the light. I sat across from her, closed blinds on the picture window blocking the sun.

"I want those two parts of you to communicate," she said.

I nodded. The whapping stopped. She reached for her notebook and pencil.

"Close your eyes."

I could still see the orange afterglow on the screen behind my eyelids, could still feel her fist hitting her palm, my ears barely registering the glide of her pencil across the paper where I imagined her writing "freak" and "Harvard?"

"Where's the little girl, Michelle"

"Hiding."

"From who?"

I shook my head.

"Where is she hiding?"

"The closet. It's dark except for the light between the door and the carpet. But this angry shadow keeps moving across the light, back and forth, back and forth."

"Whose shadow is it?"

"The mean woman. She's yelling. 'You're so stupid! You're so stupid!' And she's punching her palm with her fist."

"What does the little girl look like?"

"She's small. She'll get bigger. Next year, she'll be the tallest one in her class, but in kindergarten, she's still small and everyone looks big to her. She doesn't want to grow up. If she grows up she'll be mean."

"Tell me what else the mean woman is saying."

"You think all the shit you've done will make everything go away? It won't. I know who you are. I know what's inside you. You can cover yourself. You can scrub and scrub, but I know you're a dirty girl. You're dirty and nasty and stupid."

"Keep going," Alma said.

"She's opening the closet door now. I can see her standing above me. She's angry and strong-looking, but she's really sad. She's crying now and pulling her hair."

"Tell me what she's saying."

"It's your fault. You didn't have to follow him into the room. You knew better. You could have pushed him off. You should have told him you weren't that kind of girl. You didn't protect yourself."

"What does the little girl say back, Michelle?"

"I'm sorry. I'm sorry."

"Why is she saying she's sorry?"

"She let someone hurt her."

"Does she know it's not her fault?"

I shook my head, pulled Alma's throw pillow closer to me.

"Michelle, does she know it's not her fault?"

A small voice inside me said, "No."

"Can you tell her now?"

South / Huitzlampa | 167

My lip quivered. "It's not your fault."

"Say it again."

"It's not your fault."

"Say it again."

"I was so little. I didn't know. It's not my fault." On Alma's couch, I was five again, holding her pillow like my Raggedy Ann, tears and snot running down my face. "I never told. I didn't know. It wasn't my fault. I didn't do anything wrong."

"You did nothing wrong. It's not your fault.

"What do you need right now?"

"Water. I need to throw up. I…" I pulled my hair, wiped snot on my sleeve. "I—burn something. That picture of me. Where I'm flexing my muscles, pretending I'm strong and everything's okay."

Alma handed me the picture and a matchbook. She pushed the trashcan to my feet and placed her water glass next to it.

"Just in case," she said, shrugging.

I lit a match and touched it to one corner. That universe shriveled, first the reef, then the pier. I could almost smell the hair burning on her thighs, flames swallowing her cut-offs and tank top, the false confidence in her raised arms. The clouds above her blackened and crumbled. I poured Alma's water over the photo as heat reached my fingertips. I dropped the last corner, one water-spotted cloud, into the trashcan.

*

I leave Alma's office and drive to a park. I sit beneath a cottonwood, resting my head against its trunk. Beneath the sun, kids run through the playground, from swings to slide to monkey bars, their mothers standing watch at a nearby picnic table. They don't see her, the little girl with the striped shirt and high-water jeans. I do. She swings, her elbows hooked around the links, fingers interlaced, her head tilted back, eyes on the cloud-shapes above. She looks at me. Sweet face—hazel eyes, bangs over her eyebrows. I smile. She smiles back. When she turns to the sun, I follow her gaze. Through the cottonwood leaves, sun droplets sprinkle my bare arms and legs. A breeze grazes my face, strokes my hair like fingers. I breathe it in and close my eyes, knowing the little girl is watching.

Malinche's Daughter

My fingernail catches on a blue thread loosened from the cuff of my embroidered blouse. I yank. The white of my nail dangles, caught in the fibers of Oaxaca, the work of women's hands. It falls to the concrete floor of the room I rent from Rita.

My terrace overlooks the courtyard we share. I've spent enough mornings below to reconstruct the scene without lifting from my chair and spiraling down my private staircase into the family space. Rita scurries from the courtyard table to the kitchen to her bedroom and back, the shock of gray hair behind her ear like a cottontail, her footsteps hardly registering on the patio bricks. Her shadow follows long and thin across the two-story wall separating her home from the neighbors.

Clara turns a cartwheel to pass the time until her dad shows up to take her to the mercado, her black hair still slick and neat from the wet comb Rita ran through it at breakfast. Today is special, la víspera de Muertos. The boys watch cartoons in Rita's bedroom. They will stay with Rita this morning. Pablo says there's no room for all the kids in his car. When he and Clara return with sugar cane, pan de muerto, marigolds, and candles, we will construct an altar together and welcome the dead into this home.

The front door creaks open. Pablo shouts into the entryway, "Ya Clara. Let's go." He steps outside facing the street where he's left his Volkswagen running. Clara wipes her hands on her pink jeans and runs toward her father. He reaches over her head and closes the door.

My ring finger throbs, a horizon of blood rising from the nail bed. I shake out my hands and type the stories of my dead, my ghosts.

Pablo's sculpture, a bruise-colored imp riding a tricycle, holds open my bedroom door. Like all his creations, it's built of things that hurt children: rusted nails and keys, copper tubing cut jagged, electrical sockets, bolts and nuts.

I work with women. They find me. *She's Michelle. She helps women who suffer from violence.* Women who suffer from violence. We say it like it's a disease. *She suffers from violence.* Suffers from cancer. Arthritis.

Migraines. We don't talk perpetrators in our introductions. An acquaintance, a boyfriend, a father, a brother you love. As if the violence somehow strikes them. Strikes us. This is Rita. This is Malinche. This is Teresa, Lucía, Clara, Michelle. We suffer from violence.

I'm not a therapist or a doctor. I am a writer, a Fulbright Fellow in Oaxaca, giving writing workshops for women.

We write to heal our wounds.

*

"I think somebody...somebody did something to me." I believe the women who say this to me. The first time I heard these words it was my voice speaking. I don't remember when language came to me, but I remember my first real truth. Somebody did something to me. Remember speaking that truth aloud with a conviction and a horror I'd never experienced. I sat with my spiritual director in her office. On her bookcase, a wood carving of a ballet dancer stood in the breeze blowing through the open French doors. They sat across from me, the dancer, my spiritual director. Solid women.

"Were you sexually abused?"

I nodded.

"Your brother."

I nodded.

She nodded.

I closed my eyes, the breeze hot against my face. "I don't want to look at this."

"But here it is."

I remember nothing else she said. In memory I look up at her through water. She is above the surface. I am below. But she reaches for me, grasping my hands and pulling. Other hands, women's hands, push me from below. Mamá Malinche, her daughters. Their breath lifts me. Their words buoy me so I rise to the surface, finally able to breath.

*

I was five when someone did something to me. Now I am 33, the age of Jesus. La edad sagrada. I remembered when I was 24. I returned to a

170 | VESSELS

room, *that* room, to yellow carpet against my back. Raggedy Ann's black thread eyes staring at me, and a boy asking, "Can you feel me?"

I held that room, those words, inside me as long as I could. The pressure of secrets burst through me. Bed-wetting through third grade. Handfuls of black hair trailing me in junior high. Migraines my senior year. Acne at Harvard. And more acne. A face that hurt, almost asking the world not to touch me.

I don't want to look at this. Nobody does.

But here it is.

We write to heal our wounds.

*

When I use the Spanish word sobreviviente, people think I work with survivors of accidents, natural disasters and wars. You mean víctimas, they tell me. People nod in recognition when I use the term agresión sexual. Some know victims and want to send them to my workshops. But they wince when I say violación.

Here I've learned to soften my vocabulary—suffer from violence, sexual aggression. I've opened the workshops to all women, knowing survivors will be among them. I call the course "Writing to Heal our Wounds," a creativity workshop for women.

Even the women, especially the women, who seek me out won't say violación. Nobody will say incesto.

They don't correct me when I confuse the Spanish words for sunrise, amanecer, and threat, amenazar. I didn't grow up here. I don't know the men and boys in their stories. I help them write. I write my own story, I change names and details and speak of our work in English.

My last name is Otero. It's a Spanish name brought to the Americas by conquistadors and friars. I'm tall in Oaxaca, with wavy, black hair and a long, thin face, my eyes the shades of a forest. People ask where I am from, where my people are from. I say, "Nuevo México. El Norte." But it doesn't make sense to them. I don't make sense to them. I have no stories of crossing. The border crossed us, made us subjects, citizens of the working-class, English speaking spics, Mexican-American, Chicanos. We wander inside ourselves looking for our Tenochtitlán, our ancestral home, our Aztlán, peering as Malinche must have when she stood at

South / Huitzlampa | 171

the volcano's ledge over the city on lake Texcoco, feeling the draw of the water, knowing as they crossed the causeway that she must speak.

No one can place my accent—pocha, fronteriza, Mestiza, Chicana. Born and raised in the U.S. English at home. Spanish in college. Descendant of conquistadores and those who wouldn't be conquered. My raza's Adam and Eve are an armed Spaniard and the Mixtec, Maya, Mexica, or any other girl transferred from her cacique's hands to the Spaniards. Cortés and his men collected Eva tras Eva as they marched toward Tenochtitlán.

Maybe Adán found Eva hiding in the milpa, forced out when he set fire to the cornstalks. No. Malinche and her sisters had no place to hide, their tierra flattened by horses' hooves and marching men. Malinche's daughters did their best during the Mexican revolution—cowering in dovecotes, amongst the pigeons, or burrowing into the fecund earth, a reed connecting their mouths to breath and sky. They try to hide in Juárez's maquiladoras, or holding their mother's hand as they cross to el norte. Rita hides behind her courtyard walls. My students hide in their jobs, their routines, their unwritten pages. I once hid under my bed in dreams of men leering through windows. Here in Oaxaca, I sit high in this protected room with its private staircase and look over the terrace to the neighbors' rooftops.

Maybe a cacique exchanged Eva for protection or a false and temporary peace. They gave the bearded men with eyes like chalk golden soles for sandals and village daughters and concubines.

I've seen it in Diego Rivera's mural *The Conquest*, almost hidden between arches in the Palacio Nacional in Mexico City. A Spanish conquistador rapes a Mexica woman. Their child is my mother, my grandmother, my familia. My people—some call us "cosmic"—suffer from violence.

I straddle north and south, Spanglish running across my body from one side of the border to the other, birthing a new text between women who know too well about conquest—survivor to survivor. I bridge the United States of Mexico and America with these stories I type, these weavings of my story and theirs. My fingers, our fabric, I interpret women's stories with my hands and soul the color of canela. I am Malinche's daughter.

Mamá. I find her in Oaxaca—on the page, staring back from my reflection, in the copal smoke rising from my altar. She spoke Yucatec and Nahuatl. She learned Spanish and Jesus. And now she is silent.

She sends me women.

*

Teresa finds me first, her email waiting when I arrive in Oaxaca. We meet between the sculpted lions guarding Parque Juárez El Llano. Her full lips and cheeks seem almost too big for her face. Unless she smiles. We smile this first day, the shyness of new friends who grew up speaking different languages—Zapotec, English. We walk past the newspaper stands, past men with black-stained fingers shining shoes. We walk past women with gray braids ladling atole from stainless steel ollas they wrap in blankets and cart like children in rusted wagons. We find an empty bench along the footpaths where walkers, joggers and kids in strollers circle the park. A teenaged couple sits intertwined on the bench next to us, backpacks at their feet.

She says she wants to write. Her hair in a ponytail, she wears jeans and a T-shirt. Comfortable clothing. Clothing in which you can move. We do this for weeks. Talk of her village, her family's activism, how she quit high school and moved to the U.S. to earn dollars waitressing in a friend's restaurant and gallery in Tucson.

In our meetings, she looks down before asking a favor, making a request. She looks at her hands. I imagine husk lines on her palms. Her mud colored skin looks almost sculpted of her family's earth.

"Can you help me put it together? Can we talk someplace quieter next time?"

We meet at a museum courtyard with wooden tables and bougainvillea cascading down the cal-finished walls. She looks at her hands. It happened in Tucson. "Somebody did something to me." Really she said hacerme daño, to hurt, harm, damage. He was someone she knew, a guy who'd show up for gallery events and try to chat with her while she worked. He asked her out. She said no. He followed her home one night after a shift. She changed her schedule, changed her route. Weeks passed. One evening he followed her off the bus. She was alone in a grocery store parking lot. He dragged her to a park and raped her.

South / Huitzlampa | 173

Lucía is a university student with a face like the moon in the night sky. We come from the same desert stretching from Chihuahua through El Paso and New Mexico. Her state is the only one with more rapes than Oaxaca. In our desert, mothers find their daughters' bones disintegrating in the sun.

She is often the first to arrive. One evening as we wait for the others, she asks what I do when I'm not writing or teaching this workshop.

"I work one on one with sobrevivientes of sexual assault."

She shakes her head. "When you've been through something like that..." The others begin to arrive. I tell Lucía I am starting a group for survivors, and we should talk if she is interested or knows someone who is. And then I start the meeting, welcoming the compañeras to our circle, asking them one by one about their River of Life drawings, their journals, their creative journeys.

*

Rita is always the first to give up her chair, the first to gather plates after a meal, even if she's not the hostess. She pours hot water into my teacup even if the carafe sits closest to me.

We sometimes write together. I give her a blue journal with wire binding and a print of Monet's *Water Lilies* on the cover. She doesn't have time for the workshop. She can't afford a babysitter, and she doesn't like asking the children's father for favors. Pablo says he does enough driving Clara to school each morning—those mornings when he remembers, when he arrives on time. Some days he drives her right back, depositing her in the courtyard, her powder blue uniform jumper not even wrinkled because they arrived after eight-thirty when the doors are locked.

Pablo designed this house. He's the artist. He selected the stone virgin for the patio, the rustic bars for the courtyard windows. He placed the man-sized sculpture at Rita's bedroom door.

He doesn't live in this house. He lives with Rita's mother. This made sense when Rita lived there, too, when she still wanted Pablo to love her. I don't know what finally pushed her.

Maybe it was the hours she worked when Clara was a baby and

Pablo's art sat in his workshop rather than selling in a gallery. Monday through Saturday, three computer classes a day, eight to noon, noon to four, four to eight.

Maybe it was the art opening, his first solo show. While Rita filled the art lovers' shot glasses with mezcal, Pablo stood before his sculpture, *The Giant*, and toasted his pretty apprentice.

Maybe it was the last time he told Rita, "Put the kids to bed." And she noticed the turn, ever so slight, of her stomach, thinking of him waiting for her with his pants undone.

She thought like a reasonable person. *If I ask him to leave, he'll find his own place.*

"You're the one with the problem. You leave," he said.

She told her mother.

"Your problems with Pablo shouldn't affect the children. He might not watch them like you do, but he won't let them die."

*

Like Rita, Teresa can't attend the workshops. She waits tables and takes classes to finish high school. We meet once a week. I teach her writing. She teaches me words.

"Suéltame."

Let go of me.

Suéltame. What she told the man who grabbed her arm in a supermarket parking lot in a city far from Oaxaca, a city where she served coffee and huevos rancheros to Chicanos and white people and saved money for school.

Suéltame. She told him again when he dragged her across the asphalt and past the rows of parked cars toward a gap in the chain link fence separating the grocery store from the park.

Suéltame. She whispers it today. I don't count how many times she told him. Told him. Not yelled. She'd heard it's worse if you yell.

Once they reached the park, the cover of trees, he lifted her. It was easy. She's so small. Zapoteca-Mexicana small. The women from her village grow close to the earth. He lifted her. She lost a shoe kicking him. One shoe still in that park with its dusty trails and empty benches.

Today she wears jeans and a sweater in cobblestone shades. I've never seen her in bright colors, never seen her in a skirt. She wears boots with a city-walking tread. She could run if she had to.

"Se me encimó."

He climbed on top of her. She couldn't breathe. She tells me this as she pulls an invisible web from the slope beneath her chin. His fingers. Still squeezing.

"Me pegó."

He hit her head against the concrete picnic table. Dizzied her. She doesn't tell me how she kept from passing out. She doesn't tell me how he unzipped her pants, where she focused her eyes. She stops talking, stares at the table top—unfinished but smooth.

"Lo siento." She apologizes.

"Es que—" she wipes a tear from the inside corner of her eye, "recuerdo." She remembers. She looks up at me. Blinks her coffee-colored eyes. Twice. Once. Dry.

*

We call our circle of women sacred. There are three groups. One morning, one evening, and one afternoon. Over the twelve-week course, the women transform. Carolina cuts her hair from shoulder length to pixie. Mayté submits her poetry to a contest. Chayo takes herself to the movies. Sabina contests her ex-husband's claim for custody of their children. Three mornings a week Esther walks, then runs, the stairs up el Cerro del Fortín to Guelaguetza Stadium.

We work with pictures. Each of us writes a physical description and the apparent story behind the images. I write of two women, a mother and daughter, standing in a rose garden, their arms around each other. We write again, this time of the photo's truth.

> I spread my arms as wide as Jesus and hug my mother. There's the slightest tension in the hand I've placed on her shoulder. I can almost feel her forearm on my back. She doesn't know I'm sick, and I'll soon leave the man who holds me at night as I cry and say, "I hate my life." She can't see

176 | **VESSELS**

my scars, my fear. Even I can't see them. If not for memory, I'd believe I am simply the woman I appear to be—tall and thin with a short hairstyle you might describe as athletic, and an easy smile. When my mother goes home, I'll sleep through the afternoon and spend the night awake and silent.

When you've been through something like that...

*

I begin a workshop for sexual assault survivors with two former students, both therapists at the State Commission on Human Rights. We meet Saturdays from ten to one. Often the women don't arrive until ten-thirty, eleven, sometimes as late as twelve. We welcome them. One brings a child who plays with his Spiderman action figure as we write and puts his hand on his mother's when she cries.

Each week when we check in, Lucía smiles and says, "Things are good, really good." She nods like those bobble-head Chihuahuas on the back dashes of Mexican taxis. She's been through the course. She knows the techniques. She wanted this group more than any of the others. She's never missed a session.

We have two weeks to go, and she's asking what comes next—another workshop, individual counseling. She talks of the abuse in general terms. There was a novio. He mistreated her. She got out. Here she is. Someday she'll be a lawyer and put people like him in jail.

A pillar candle sits in the center of our circle. Watercolors, crayons, magazines, scissors and glue bottles lie around it. A bouquet of Mylar balloons with smiling cartoon birds in assorted colors and shapes hovers over me, their red ribbons tied to my folding chair.

I will facilitate after the balloon ritual. Right now, it's my colleague who talks of letting go and transformation.

"We've spent eleven weeks together. We've shared our stories. We've gotten angry. We've cried. We've acknowledged the people who hurt us. In the second half of the meeting, we'll create altars honoring our lives.

But now it's time to release the responsibility and guilt we've carried.

"Write a letter to your aggressor. Write what you need to say in this moment."

Lucía grinds a fingernail between her teeth before settling into her words. Her chipped nail guides the pen. I like the sounds of pain turning to ink, drying upon the page.

I don't write to my brother. He apologized long ago when the memories were new. He asked me to breakfast. I wanted to say no, to wander alone beneath the branches of desert willows and fruitless mulberries, to feel the leaves crack beneath my running shoes. Back then I thought if I closed my eyes I could erase the memory. I wonder how I saw anything at all.

"You can write the letter however you'd like. In the voice of the person you were or the person you are now, or both. You can use real names, or you can invent a name. Your letter can be as short or as long as you need it to be in this moment."

Where do you go once you've written that letter? I am luckier than most. This I know.

The boy who hurt me took responsibility. But what do I do with the residue, with the pieces I still carry?

I write to myself. I am the aggressor I must face, the one who continues to damage me. I weigh the men I've chosen. An artist who painted me ugly on purpose. A photographer who clipped my toenails and made them beautiful in black and white. I have loved the extremes. An artist who wouldn't touch me at all. A photographer who wouldn't stop.

I don't cry in this space. Here there is no room for my story. I am the Teacher.

As each woman finishes, we hand her a balloon and help her tie the letter to the ribbon. Lucía finishes last. Her words fold thick, sinking the yellow cartoon bird to our chests.

We go outside.

I release my balloon. I feel my spirit lifting with the reflective star as it clears the chain link fence, the power lines across the street, the razor wire around the baseball stadium. I don't think of it coming down again, far from me.

Lucía's balloon won't lift over our heads. She ties another to the letter then casts it all toward the sky. The heart and circle clear the fence and catch on a utility post. We should have done this in an open field, should have given these words every shot of getting away. We stand watching, nobody speaking. We inhale with each puff of wind and sigh as the balloons remain fixed.

We walk back inside to make our altars. I tell Lucía the wind and rain will erode her letter and wash her words clean. She smiles and nods and says she knows, but she looks out the window every few minutes, grinding the same fingernail between her teeth.

A week later, one balloon still hangs from the post, the yellow bird on its metallic surface smiling upside down.

*

Tonight Pablo sits across from me at the courtyard table, Clara asleep in his arms. Even dressed up, almost elegant in his gray coat, he always looks unkempt, his hands cracked and stained a different shade depending on the material he employs—lacquer, ashes, axle grease, paint. He always needs a shave, and his curly black hair either frizzes or sets unevenly under gel.

He talks about a boy Clara likes in her first grade class. Pablo wonders whether to approach the boy, to invite his father out for a beer. "I want her to trust me with these things," he says. "¿Y tú, Michelle? ¿Qué opinas?"

"¿Qué opino yo?" I ask, taking a deep breath. "I think she's six years old."

"Pues, sí. Claro."

He tells me about his work, his sculptures, how one of these days I should go with him to the dump or to junkyards or dumpsters to look for material. He has his favorite places, places he's told no one about. He tells me I should write about him. Rita pours coffee and heats more water for my tea.

He invites me to his workshop.

I don't tell him I've been through his space alone. It was Clara's birthday. While she complained to her parents, *You said it was my party, you said there would be kids*. I left the porch and walked to his shed in back.

South / Huitzlampa | 179

His workshop. Chicken wire. A blowtorch he uses to solder without a mask or safety goggles. Washers, spark plugs, olive oil drums with a Spanish maiden on the label. Carburetors. Everything covered by a thin layer of grease. Or you feel like it should be. Broken mirrors and window glass. Kitchen utensils bent as if by fire. Rusted bicycle chains, aluminum can pull-tabs, gutted beer cans. And further in, a dingy cot with a wire stretched above it. In a cleaner place it might be a clothesline. Here, instead of white shirts or handkerchiefs, naked Barbie dolls hang from the line. Some smiling, string knotted around their necks. Others headless, hooks protruding from their necks holding them to the line. No hair between their thighs. Like little girls.

Pablo puts Clara to bed and leaves. Rita sits across from me. She tells me about that night, Clara's birthday.

"Pablo said he'd drive us home."

So she drank and danced and couldn't remember the last time he'd been so nice to her, the last time he'd touched her hair, her face. They kissed at stoplights. The children slept in the backseat. As they passed the park, the lions at the entrance forever awake in stone, she drifted. Pablo put them to bed one by one.

"I don't know what happened," she tells me. "When I got up to make breakfast, Clara was in bed with me. Pablo was in the extra room sleeping. His pants were unzipped, but they were still on. You came downstairs. Do you remember?"

I do.

As Rita drank her coffee that morning, Pablo and I talked of my book, his exhibit. I folded an empty sugar packet in halves against the table, creasing with the pad of my index finger until I couldn't fold anymore, adding this pebble to the others in the table crack. Pablo moved his chair closer to Rita. He stroked her neck, her hair, circling his finger in her shock of gray. I'd never seen him touch her like that. He seemed handsome, almost tender. She nose-dived, slowing her momentum in time to tap her forehead against the table. It seemed to stick.

"Look at my Rita, Michelle."

She perched her chin on the table, her head framed by the bars on the window behind her. "Isn't she beautiful?" Pablo asked.

Her mouth was like a mask attached by string, the corners so rigid, set so far into her jaw her lips almost disappeared.

"So pretty." He pet her hair.

"You finished your coffee and went upstairs to write. Do you remember?" Rita's question jars me back to the dark courtyard.

I nod.

Once they were alone, he leaned closer and told her, "Last night was lo mejor. I've never done it to anyone like that."

"Is it agresión if I don't remember?" Without waiting for my answer, she says, "If it is, better me than Clarita."

*

Clara, Clarita. When she grows up, men will call her intensa.

If I lived alone with her, or if she were my blood sister, I'd squat down to face her, my hands her shoulders, my brown face so close to hers my wet breath would mist tips of her black, matte-finished hair.

Who hurt you, little girl?

When I meet her she is five.

Now you are six, Clarita. You draw me a woman with a belly and entitle it, *And She Got Pregnant.* You are too often sick. Fever. Nightmares. Headaches. You whisper to me, *I have a boyfriend,* a chubby boy in your first-grade class. *Don't tell my mom.* He chased you at a birthday party. You wrote his number on your palm and kept your hand in a fist so your mom wouldn't notice, didn't wash that hand after using the bathroom, and because you were dirty, you refused pastel de tres leches, your favorite cake. You undress your girl doll and lie the boy doll on top of her, his denims bunched at his plastic knees. I glance at them, lying there on the breakfast table, next to my plate of papaya and watermelon. And when I look up, you are staring at me with those eyes so dark and intense they seem painted and polished in oils. I ask your girl doll's name.

"She doesn't have one."

When your dad visits, you stand next to him and talk to nobody else. When he leaves I ask you why.

"He gets sad if I talk to you."

He hugs her too close. Enjoys it too much. Touches her hair like a lover.

"Isn't my Clara beautiful?" And then he smiles. Like he made her beauty. Like it exists only because he saw it. Touched it. The look on her face is part hunger, part nausea in the courtyard with high walls the color of papaya flesh, with bars on the window behind her, with the heavy wooden door she can't open alone, the door to which her father owns a key.

Sometimes she leaves his side and turns cartwheels in the patio or shows him her handstand. He turns to her mother and me.

"Look how my Clara's growing," he says. He turns back to the child, bites the skin around his thumbnail. "Her legs are so pretty." He bites. "She's got a nice little shape."

And she is beautiful. The way summer storms are beautiful.

I sometimes watch her from my terrace. She is my muertos ghost. Not a kind soul who fills my room with warm light, but a llanto whose song reflects my deepest pain. She cries from the edge of the human voice, like men dying in battle.

She asks her mother, "What was I like?" She wants stories of her childhood—as if it no longer exists. Tell her of a time before now.

Those are questions I've asked my mother. *Tell me how I was before age five.* I know Clara has to go back further. Beyond the womb, to Chichihuacuauhco, the Place of the Nipple Tree, where Mexica souls feed while waiting to be born. I want to carry her there, give her to Mamá Malinche, and let us all begin anew.

It's night in the courtyard. Rita and I drink manzanilla.

"Pablo says Clarita will choose violent men because she grew up without a dad," she says, lifting the carafe and filling my cup with hot water. "What do you think?"

I suck in my breath. I soften my language. "I think Clara's relationship with her father does her damage."

Rita looks at me, then darts her eyes around the courtyard as if scanning for disaster. She pinches the gray in her hair between her thumb and forefinger.

"The way he touches her hair. What he says about her body."

She closes her eyes.

I tell her. I tell her about the night Clara slept in the backseat of the car. Her father was drunk. It was Christmas Eve. We waited to drive to Tío's house for dinner and gifts while Rita ran inside for the kids' pajamas and Pablo smoked in the cold between the car and the streetlight. He flicked the cigarette to sidewalk, opened the car door, and pulled the bucket seat forward.

"Ay Clara," he said. She slept. He leaned toward her. "So pretty, my Clarita." Closer. She slept. And then, as though he fainted, as though the weight of his head was suddenly too much, he fell onto his daughter, his forehead just under her bellybutton, his nose between her six-year-old legs. An instant. She slapped him away with both hands as if dog-paddling. He laughed.

"Pinche Clara," he said, laughing. Laughing, as if to say, *Isn't it cute the way she fights back? She thinks she can win.*

*

Teresa will take a job out of town. I will leave Rita's house for my own apartment. I start a workshop for incest survivors. Nobody comes. Each week, I am forced to look at myself, to look home, to see my reflection in that mirrored balloon still hanging from a power line between the baseball field and the Human Rights parking lot.

I write of her as though she's another woman. She is me. But I am tired of those words—I, sexual, abuse, me—tired of the story they tell. I drop the words behind me, one by one, a trail of red petals covered in dust from la frontera to Guadalupe's feet at Tepayac to Oaxaca. But if I want to come home, I must follow the same path, retracing my story in red petals along the way, another layer added to it, the dust of other women's steps.

Michelle the Teacher. We write to heal our wounds. She is me.

If she were dead you'd build her an altar. You'd find her favorite things—a journal with unlined pages, marigolds, chocolate. You'd place her photo on top and remember. They called her the smiling woman, la bella Michelle. You'd make a sand painting of Guadalupe on her gravestone and you'd sit with her through the night, missing her and thankful you are not in her place.

There is no gravestone for her, for them, except the one inside her or on the page where she writes and writes the names of all the women who have said "me too," when she's told her story. Each name, each story, nicks her soul, opens it as wide as the blank page.

Years ago, when the memories were new, her eyelid twitched. Red vessels crossed the whites of her eyes, mapping the landscape of her nightmares. She slept eight, sometimes nine, ten hours a night but woke exhausted, her head and muscles heavy.

She writes these dreams in a spider script, holds her notebook open for me to see.

> I hear a car engine, the creak of a door, a slam. I separate the blinds with my thumb and index finger. A shaft of gray light enters my bedroom. Two men, giants with hands the size of baseball gloves, dwarf the car, a compact. It's blue. The men wear browns and grays and blacks, everything faded and too small. They are wider than my doorframe and to enter they must crouch and squeeze. They glance at me, then look past me. Without words or effort, they hoist my bed above their shoulders and carry it into a gray sky.

Dreams mark the years for her, the healing steps. They say what she cannot. She shares another dream only in the silence of written words, in journal pages she wants cremated with her so flesh and word will be one.

> I stand in my brother's bedroom, hands at my sides. It is night. Light seems to rise from the floor, as though the yellow carpet is a lantern or a blanket of candles licking my fingertips. Shadow spills from the ceiling like dust. I drift through the room. My arm brushes against familiar fabric. I touch the hem of polyester slacks, a denim cuff, the elastic of cotton sweatpants. The ceiling cracks. My fingers glide down first to my mother's pumps, next a few steps to my father's work boots, then to my brother's

running shoes. Their feet dangle above the light, their soles swallowing the glow.

I step back. In the shadows I can't see their eyes. But I know they are frozen, forever looking away from me. I see only shapes: meat hooks bolted to the ceiling, rope looped around each hook, and at the end of each rope, a body—father, mother, brother. Next to me a man whose face I won't remember gathers the remaining rope, looping it from hand to elbow.

"Who did this?" I ask him.

"You did. You shouldn't have said anything."

She is me. We follow a red trail back from Mamá Malinche, back to a five-year-old girl who weighs too much, back to a woman afraid to carry or release her, back to paper doll calaveras of women stretched across the Chihuahuan desert. We are all Malinche's daughters.

Michelle the Teacher. She returns to New Mexico. She talks to her mother.

"I'm writing about the abuse."

"I wondered if you would do that someday." They walk together at dusk. A desert bird of paradise twists up from a bed of gravel, yellow pistils pushing through the red petals like tongues. "Have you talked to your brother?"

I shake my head. I say I softened my language in Oaxaca, but I practiced for years in this desert where I was raised, paved over the hole scraped into me.

We walk up the asphalt trail snaking out of this pit that grows darker as the sun returns to earth. A family of quail crosses the path in front of us, running as though to keep their feet from burning.

"This story makes no sense without my story."

"But you're my children," she says.

We are.

And I am Malinche's daughter.

I write, run, stretch, sleep, my balance wary. I fear a slip: a week without yoga, less than eight hours of sleep, talking before writing, coffee on an empty stomach, pasta for lunch, high fructose corn syrup, Mercury in retrograde, second-hand smoke, and needy people. Especially men, all of whom say they are artists, most of whom offer to paint me. I dream of going to them unshaven and naked when I'm on my period. *Paint me now. This is the kind of woman I am. A hairy, wild—some might say savage—woman with blood dripping down her legs. Paint with that.*

I want to write pretty emails to my parents. They want me happy. *Oaxaca is faaaabulous.* I want to get up and make coffee. I want to fall away, like Teresa, go back to a time of not knowing, of simply accepting myself as fearful and too intense, as someone who both lives out of deficit and wants too much. Want to return to a time before I scrutinized my reflection, before I saw myself in Clara's black eyes, in the shock of gray hair behind Rita's ear, the white space on my students' pages, the tear Teresa blinks away, the chip in Lucía's fingernail. All together they construct a woman incomplete. I fear the process of putting myself back together will hurt too badly and in the end water will continue to seep from me. Weeping woman. Combativa. Complicada. Intensa. Silent. Beautiful. Invisible.

But I stay at the desk, my fingers limping, looking over the courtyard wall because I want to taste the next story that bleeds from me.

Dream

Grandma is a healer operating out of a one-room adobe in the desert. Pilgrims clump near her open doorway, where a pale-yellow sheet hangs from nails. She takes no appointments. Spirit moves her to determine who she'll see and in what order. I watch her through a window. She dances barefoot in a flowered cotton skirt, her hair in a loose-woven scarf. She lays her hands on a white woman's shoulders, and the woman begins to dance and speak in tongues. The woman's lover joins. They hold hands and dance in a circle. Grandma sees me out of the corner of her eye and nods toward me.

I wait.

When the ritual ends, Grandma greets the two men standing next to me. I want to tell them she is more than a healer. She's my grandma. She was dead, and now she's a healer.

She puts her hand on my elbow and guides me into the house. As soon as we are out of the men's field of vision, I hug her. She squeezes me. I don't let go.

"Grandma," I plead into her shoulder, "please come back. We need you so much."

She releases me and whispers, "You will find peace in the presence of spirit and children."

But I don't really like kids.

Instructions for January 3, 2005
winter—one year after

Cast seventy-six stones, one for each of her years, into the sea.

    Fast sun to sun.
    Find a strong chest to hold. You are so big in Oaxaca.
    Find her people, the place where her grandparents are buried and taste the dirt covering their bones. Wet their polvo with spit and paste over your own eyes. Rinse. Do not go into the village. Do not tell anyone.
    Sit in the courtyard in Mitla. This is how time passes.

afraid to feel too good too soon
- depression

what if the meds stop working
- anxiety

Fight with my Oaxaca novio who calls me by a nickname

¿Sabes, Micky? I think you hate men.

What happened in El Paso

He smoked and I coughed.
He drank and my liver scarred.
He burned through me.

Malinche. Michelle. We are survivors. We don't want to be anymore. Surely we deserve to live.

Sky

energía del universo,
donde se encuentran las cuatro direcciones

Siguiendo los Pasos de Malinche
Coatzacoalcos—where the serpent hides

The man next to me in the front passenger seat of the first class bus fell asleep before we pulled away from the terminal. I had wanted the window so I could have something to lean my head against for the overnight trip from Oaxaca to the state of Veracruz. Instead I stared from my aisle seat out the front window at the torta and taco puestos across from the terminal, the jacarandas dividing our traffic lanes from theirs, everything interrupted by the heads of the driver and his co-pilot who sat on a wooden stool he'd pick up and tuck under his arm each time we stopped for more passengers.

There was no direct bus from Oaxaca City to Coatzacoalcos, so instead I headed south five hours to Salina Cruz on a winding divided highway, passing freight trucks and fruit trees, coffee plantations, sights I could only imagine in the darkness. I'd switch buses on the Oaxacan coast and then head north and east another six hours to Coatzacoalcos, an industrial city, the place where the feathered serpent Quetzalcóatl promised to return, where Malinche's journey with Cortés and the Spaniards began.

I wore a prayer bracelet made of hand-carved beads strung together by my friend Michele, an artist and writer who'd been living in Oaxaca for ten years. The beads were a soft light brown wood. When she gave me the bracelet at dinner she twisted and doubled the string around my wrist so the largest bead of each string interlinked to form a crude heart or maybe a vulva at the base of my palm. I worried the amulet like a stone, infusing my prayers, my hopes for this trip, which I'd put off as long as possible, spending more time in Oaxaca than I should have. I had moved back to the US more than a year earlier to finish graduate school and pay off my loans, but I still wanted Oaxaca to be my home. I didn't know how to live in Mexico without a fellowship or graduate school loans. I'd fantasized about finding a wealthy Mexican novio who'd provide for me and let me write. There had been a wealthy Mexican, someone who adored me, said he loved me. He had his own house on his family's land, where he said I could write and finish my book. *Yo te cuido.* And though I'd wanted to love him, even now I wanted to love him, I didn't. I didn't love him in my bones. I didn't love him the way I wanted to love and be loved.

We passed the turn off to El Tule and its fifteen-hundred-year-old ahuehuete, where schoolchildren in green and white uniforms point out animal shapes in its branches with hand mirrors, reflecting sunlight onto el venado, el león, el jaguar.

The bus downshifted as we reached a mountain pass. Banda music, with its oom-pah horns, played over the stereo. If this were a day bus, the music would be blasting, and we'd get a movie on the screens mounted above every third seat.

I wished for a movie now, something to distract me. A part of me was waiting for someone to save me, to get me unstuck, to say *I'll take care of you* and *I'll take care of it*, all the *it*—my loans, the car payment my brother had stopped making, paperwork, finding a source of income in Oaxaca, or not needing one, accepting me, really seeing me and wanting me anyway. A bigger part of me said I had to save myself, to fix what was broken inside me before I could be loved.

I thought of all the friends supporting me, the people who believed in me, the email from a writer friend: *You know those women you help out? What if you gave some of that to yourself?*

Had I? Had I helped? There are women writing together now because they came to know each other in my workshops. There are women who are friends now because they met in my workshops. There are women teaching other women to write now. There are women who are less isolated now. I helped. And I was helped along the way. This is what community does.

There was the healer I called in desperation before this trip: *Do you really think God would bring you this far just to drop you?*

Well, yeah. I do.

My book had put a rift between my family and me. Conversations with my parents were strained. Though the book wasn't about them, my brother and sister-in-law hadn't talked to me, or maybe I hadn't talked to them, in over a year. I hadn't told them what I was writing. Or I had. I'd tried. I'd read a section—not *the* section—out loud around their dining room table. My mom said, "It's beautiful." My sister-in-law said, "It's hard for me to get it just hearing it out loud. I'd have to read it on paper." I'd sent a chapter to my brother. He never responded. I didn't know how to prepare them. I only knew I needed to write. I needed their help and didn't know how to ask for it. I was afraid they'd tell me no, and if they did, then I wouldn't know what or how to write.

The drivers chatted. The man next to me snored. I slipped off my clogs and took a pair of wool socks out of my backpack. I rolled up the light rebozo I usually saved for summers and put it between my lower back and the seat. My layers—a pair of black leggings, a black camisole with built in bra, and a red cotton pullover—felt too bulky for packing light and too thin to protect me from the air conditioner, much less the colder temperatures I'd find in Mexico City where my trip would culminate in a little more than a week.

I couldn't sleep. On paper my project excited me—retrace Malinche's steps with the Spaniards from point of contact to Mexico City, time my arrival in the city with the Feast Day of Our Lady of Guadalupe. I didn't know how to research. I wasn't searching archives or talking with experts. My quest for Malinche resembled my search for love. I was convinced if my heart was open, if I were sincere, I would be led to the right people and places.

They—he—would cross my path without my forcing a thing.

Except for Mexico City, where my friend Rosa María had arranged for us to meet at the bus terminal and travel to her friend's apartment, I didn't have people waiting in any of these cities. I was afraid, not of harm or strangers, but of loneliness, of failure, of not recognizing success or of resting too readily in coincidences, in gut feelings and serendipity—the clerk at Librería Educal who pointed me to *Ecos de la Conquista*, based on the writings of the conquistador Bernal Díaz del Castillo and the Franciscan friar Bernardino de Sahagún; the friend who happened to have an extra cell phone in his truck and offered it to me as he drove me to the bus station; Michele wrapping the prayer bracelet around my wrist the moment I was feeling untethered. So many people had invested in me: a foundation in New Mexico, a fund for women writers, the friend who gave me the spare room in her casita and said *stay as long as you need*, the other friend who hired me to housesit when she and her husband traveled out of the country.

How did I feel so alone?

I had written two winning proposals, and yet, I didn't know enough about Malinche or Cortés to retrace their steps. My route had been mapped out on a bar napkin a few nights earlier by a buddy of the adoring, wealthy Mexican. The buddy was fascinated by Malinche and Cortés, read everything he could about them, studied them in his spare time. He understood what I was trying to do, even if I didn't.

No one would be waiting for me in Coatzacoalcos, or anywhere. Not even Malinche, who I magically thought would put women in my path to guide me. It was a journey of faith, but I had none.

I hadn't slept well on this trip. I was fighting off a cold. Though the bus wound through the mountains, the road wasn't particularly winding or treacherous, and still my stomach churned. My mouth watered. A sour taste settled at the back of my throat. My hands tingled. *I'm going to throw up. I'm going to throw up, and I won't make it to the bathroom in time.* I yanked off my red pullover and held it like an airplane bag up to my mouth. I heaved as quietly as I could. The man next to me hadn't moved the entire trip, and though I'd wanted the window seat, now I was thankful I didn't have to climb over him to reach the aisle. I sat, rolled my pullover into a ball, felt it warm on my lap. I made myself inhale and exhale slowly to be sure it had passed, and once warmth returned to my hands, I walked the length of the bus to the bathroom, holding my shirt of vomit like an ugly child. I offered my shirt to the trash can and knelt before the bus toilet, blue water sloshing in the stainless-steel bowl. My stomach was empty. I wept. I was alone on a dark bus in Mexico and I'd hurled into my most comfortable shirt. What was I doing here? Who did I think I would find?

*

Back at my seat, I wrapped the prayer necklace around my wrist. I ran my fingers over the soft wooden beads, dipped the tip of my finger into the amulet covering my pulse. I tried to conjure the many rosaries I had attended as an offering to the dead throughout my life, the white noise drone of prayer voices *santificado sea tu nombre…bendito es el fruto de tu vientre…ruega por nosotros pecadores…* Ritual. Prayers to lift a departed soul past purgatory and into heaven.

It's always seemed an unfair gamble to me, to leave the weight of one's soul, the swiftness with which it ascends, up to the living with our jobs, our worries, our kitchens to clean, our beds to make. The last rosary I prayed was my grandmother's. The last mass I attended was her funeral. There are many reasons I don't go to church, but one is simple messaging. Couldn't my prayers be offered as communion, a way of being in touch with my grandmother? Why must it be punitive? Why must it always be that we are not enough? *If your grandma gets stuck in purgatory, it's your fault. You're not devoted/faithful/holy/good enough.* What is enough?

I woke to beads hitting and rolling across the floor, to the string that held them loose at my wrist, and more and more beads dropping under the sleeping man's feet, down the aisle toward the bathroom where my red shirt festered in the trash can. I don't know how the bracelet snapped, but by the time I staunched the break, it was more than half gone, spread throughout the bus with each tilt and turn in the road.

*

As soon as I opened my eyes to the rain-soaked bus terminal I knew I would not be spending the night. Coatzacoalcos was not lime-washed casitas with red tile roofs. It was suburban sprawl, strip malls, industrial parks. The words of the guide book I'd checked out from the library came back to me, "There's no good reason to visit Coatzacoalcos other than taking a stretch break en route to the Olmec heads further south."

It was six in the morning.

*

The bathroom attendant handed me a portion of toilet paper in exchange for three pesos. First-class bus station restrooms in Mexico are uniformly spotless with shiny tile floors that could function as mirrors. Though they never have toilet seats, they've all been scoured and mopped with Fabuloso, Pine Sol, or Cloralex. I wiped my armpits with the damp washcloth I'd packed in a ziplock bag and applied a fresh coat of deodorant. I changed into a black tank top and turquoise peasant skirt. The taste of vomit still crept at the back of my throat, so I flossed and brushed my teeth and tongue. I rinsed my face and neck, patted myself dry, and slathered myself in sunscreen. Even in these first few hours of sunlight I could already feel the heaviness of the air.

I transferred my water bottle, sunblock, laptop, journal, passport, money belt, pen, and rebozo to my saddlebag. Everything else—clothing for the next two weeks, tennis shoes, *Ecos de la Conquista*, and toiletries stayed in my duffel. The saddlebag converted into a boxy backpack, which I strapped onto my shoulders. I walked my travel pack and tote bag to Guardaequipaje. The other passengers from my bus were long gone. The terminal was quiet. The young man who unloaded our bus sat on a stool next to the bag storage counter. Despite the humidity and hours he'd already worked this morning, the collar on his white shirt was crisp, and there wasn't a hint of perspiration on his face. His short black hair was slicked back off his face. He looked up as I approached.

"Buenos días. ¿Podría dejar mis maletas?"

"Es que 'stá cerrado ahorita. Llega la gerente a las ocho y media."

Eight thirty was ninety minutes from now, and the day was only getting hotter. I didn't want to wait to leave my bags, and I couldn't fathom hauling them along the beach or malecón.

"¿Hay algún lugar en que podría dejar mis cosas hasta que llegue?" I asked, hoping he would say I could leave my things with him.

"Pués, realmente, no hay, pero..." He took a deep breath. I smiled at him, trying to look both confident and desperate at the same time. "Bueno. Sí, está bien."

"Le agradezco mucho. Muchísimas gracias."

There's a level of trust among strangers in Mexico that I don't experience in the United States. I slip into it easily each time I visit. Leaving my bags with strangers in bus terminals, holding a baby for a mother who has to use the bathroom, sharing a meal with desconocidos in the mercado or a café. I am saddened and shocked each time I return to the States, suspicion awaiting me as soon I attempt to cross back to the country of my birth, whether it's Immigration and Customs at George H.W. Bush Airport in Houston or the Bridge of the Americas linking Ciudád Juárez to El Paso.

*

A taxista dropped me off on the malecón in front of a concrete replica of Quetzalcóatl's pyramid. Two teenage girls sat in the shade cast by the feathered serpent atop the replica. I smiled at the girls, imagining their friendship built on early morning talks along the ocean. I missed my friends, my rituals. I wanted someone to ride the bus with me, to help me make decisions, to remind me to pack the sunglasses I'd left in Oaxaca. My stomach growled. It was Sunday morning. The restaurants across the street hadn't yet opened for the day.

I looked to the sea, expecting Cortés's ship to appear on the surface.

Footsteps slapped up the steps on the other side of the monument. Soon a boy and girl about five or six raced around to my side. Behind them, slower, an older doughy boy in flip flops called behind him, "¡Ven, 'má!" A woman in white slacks and heels came around the corner and took his arm. "Sí, mi amor, stá bonita." Her hair was pulled back in a chignon, and her lips were perfectly painted in rosa mexicano. She looked more ready for mass than for a walk along the beach, and yet, I'd seen Mexican women climb pyramids and glide across cobblestone streets in heels, their rebozos like capes. The boy and girl ran around and up and down the monument. I wondered where her pareja was, if she had one, if she had time or interest for marriage or love. The family left and piled into a car. Maybe they would go to church or breakfast. Maybe this was a stop on a road trip.

The teenagers had walked away without my noticing. A man leaned into the wall and looked toward the sea through binoculars. He left and walked along the beach. I don't know how long I stood there, breathing in the ocean, breathing through my anxiety, convincing myself I was exactly where I needed to be. I didn't know where I was going. At least I had tickets on a first-class bus, a cell phone in case of emergency, a fellowship to support me. I had come to Coatzacoalcos because *Ecos de la Conquista* said this is where Malinche was born. Coatzacoalcos, the place where the serpent hides, the place where Quetzalcóatl, the feathered serpent deity, said he would return.

The shade had shrunk to a rectangle the size of my backpack. I left my post on the seaside and walked to the other side of the monument, facing the street.

A car pulled up to a hotel across the street and two long blocks from the pyramid. A man got out and ran up the steps and into the lobby. I needed coffee and eggs. I needed a woman's kitchen and a big table to sit

sky | 203

and talk about my project and fears and the miracles in my life. I needed a curandera or a grandmother, an older sister or tía. There would be no one to talk to at the restaurant, but at least I'd be out of the sun. I could eat, drink some water, plan my day. I put on my backpack. The laptop inside weighed more like a typewriter and was almost as useless with its limited storage and no wi-fi capability. I crossed the street to a sidewalk running along a bank of hotels in full sun. I hadn't brought a hat. Not even eight in the morning, and the air was already thick, the sun heavy.

*

A mother and her adolescent son sat at the table next to mine. She opened the basket of corn tortillas on their table and put one on his plate. He put a forkful of frijoles with egg into his mouth without acknowledging her or the tortilla. She dipped a spoon into the sugar bowl and was about to mix it into his coffee cup when he picked up the cup and drank from it. She followed the cup with her eyes, from his lips to the edge of the table where he set it, as far from her as possible. She looked at the unspent sugar in her spoon and emptied it onto the paper napkin next to her plate. The boy looked at his plate until it was clean, looking up only to turn away from his mother and stare at the sea. I wondered when the boy started hating his mother. I wondered about the father and pictured him living with his other family in the capital. Or maybe this was the other family, la casa chica, la capilla en vez de la catedral. But no, this woman with gray at her temples and a straight back no matter her son's indifference had the air of wife and mother about her, of stability and its shadow, obligation.

I thought of men, men and their mothers, men and their wives, young men being raised by women. I thought of how many times in Mexico I'd been asked, *¿Eres feminista, Michelle?* and how the question always made me feel I had something to hide, how so many men had asked why my writing workshops were only for women. *¿Los hombres no tienen heridas? ¿Los hombres no merecen sanar?*

"No, no es así. Es que…" I'm tired of healing men.

My food arrived. Huevos a la Mexicana, frijoles negros, café con leche, tortillas. I ate slowly. I ate everything. I cleaned the plate with my tortilla.

I wanted to stay at the table and read or write in my journal. The thought of the day, the journey ahead, how ill-prepared I was, doing it all alone, nobody knowing where I would be day to day, the long walk to anyplace interesting, the laptop on the chair next to mine, the books in my tote bag, exhausted me. And underneath it all was my shame—for not being better prepared, for feeling afraid, for beating myself up about my lack of preparation and fear. But I asked for my bill, left sixty pesos in a basket on the table, gathered my things, and walked back to the pyramid.

The man with the binoculars was back.

He nodded at me and gestured toward the water. "Águila," he said, handing me the binoculars. Águila. I remembered Ricardo. We'd met el 16 de septiembre my first month in Oaxaca. He named me Jacinta because Michelle was not a Mexican-enough name for me. He told me a story about an eagle.

"¿Qué quiere decir águila?"

"Jacinta, no, no puede ser. ¿Cómo que no sabes?"

How could I not know this most Mexican of words. Águila. Eagle. I tried to explain. *Es que—my parents didn't teach me, por racismo, por la frontera, por los Estados Unidos.* I couldn't explain. I didn't know the words for colonization, legacy, inheritance; only shame, loss. He hugged me. He kissed my forehead.

"Yo te veo, Jacinta."

"Gracias," I said, smiling as I took the binoculars and brought them to my eyes. I've never been good with binoculars. I've never understood how to take the big sky under which we live and focus it down to an eagle gliding over the ocean. "No la veo," I said, shrugging my shoulders and handing him the binoculars. "Espera," he said, taking them. "Ahora sí." He motioned for me to stand in his spot. He held the binoculars steady while I looked through them.

The eagle glided above the water.

"Que maravilla. Gracias. Le agradezco."

"¿De dónde eres?" he asked.

"Nuevo México, Estados Unidos."

"¿Andas de vacacciones?"

I shook my head. "Soy escritora. Estoy investigando el tema de la conquista, siguiendo los pasos de Cortés y la Malinche."

"Interesante."

"¿Y usted?"

"Soy de aquí. Soy ingeniero para Pemex."

The national petroleum company was the reason Coatzacoalcos existed. I realized the vessel I'd mistaken for a barge was actually an oil tanker.

"Por ahí hay un punto en que puedes ver toda la playa y el mar," he said, pointing to one end of the malecón. "El mercado queda unas cuadras de aquí. Y a la vuelta hay un restaurante con el pescado más sabroso del estado."

"A poco," I answered, tempted by the thought of a market, which must have a juice stand and tarps for shade, by the thought of sitting at a restaurant on the water with ceviche and a margarita. My shoulders already ached, imagining the walk in the hot sun, my backpack growing heavier with every step.

"Si quieres, te podría dar un tour. Tengo moto," he said, gesturing to a motorcycle parked on the street.

I hesitated.

"Con toda la confianza," he said. I had heard the phrase before and had since taken it to mean, "Don't worry. Trust me." But, much like its English counterpart, the phrase often had the opposite effect on me, as it was usually stated by people unworthy of my trust.

Nobody knows where I am. Nobody I know could identify me based on what I am wearing today. My parents don't have my itinerary.

How far I had come since my book release more than a year earlier. I used to call my mom every time I traveled. She knew where I was from day to day, and a part of me wondered if she could still sense my exact location in the world, a kind of maternal GPS that would lead her to me if there was ever a need. I was approaching the second Christmas in a row without my parents or siblings. Is it possible to walk so far from the people who know us, to stretch so tight and thin the thread connecting us that it snaps when we try to walk back along it?

I wanted more than anything to ride on his motorcycle, to spend the day hearing about his family, to accept this blessing that befalls good travelers. More importantly, I wanted to not walk. My back hurt from the trip and from hauling my seven-year-old laptop. The canvas straps of my tote bag had already rubbed a red mark into my shoulder. The sun was fierce, and the breeze, though pleasant and kind along the water and from where we stood at the temple, did not extend across the street where the tired restaurants and hotels along the boulevard shaded the sidewalk.

I didn't know what to do. Rejecting his offer would mean I am mistrustful, anxious, judgmental, a bitch. Accepting would make me a free spirit. But if I said yes and he hurt me, then I'd be stupid for trusting a strange man.

But I did know. I felt a calm in my chest and stomach. And I trusted my knowing. I knew he wouldn't hurt me. I knew he was exactly what he appeared to be. A middle-aged father, a husband, a man who attends mass near the mercado every Sunday, a person who wanted to share what he loved about the place he called home.

I got on his motorcycle.

Siguiendo los Pasos de Malinche
journal

Veracruz

Hotel on the zócalo. Elevator operated by an elderly man in a white guayabera. Hungry. Congested.

I ask the clerk in the zócalo bookstore where I can find a caldo de 7 mares. He points me to a hole in the wall on a plazuela where a stage is set up and a man dressed as a clown speaks into a microphone. *Sí. Sí. Sí. Probando. Uno. Dos. Tres.*

The soup is medicine, home, a warm bed, my grandma's kitchen, and my favorite blanket all in one. I want to crawl into the bowl and live there until my health is fully restored.

Clowns come in and out all evening, drinking water at the bar, chatting with the waiter, touching up their makeup in the bathroom, as children's music plays on the plazuela.

Danzón and orchestra in the zocalo.

I'm still congested the next day, but at least rested. I join a guided tour of San Juan de Ulúa, an island fortress. It's been a presidential palace, a naval base, and a prison. The cells are dank, cave-like, stalactites dripping from the ceiling.

Cortés met here with Moctezuma's emissaries, Tendile and Pitalpitoque on Easter Sunday 1519.

The guide points out el puente de los suspiros, which prisoners would cross on their way to execution. Seems there's always a bridge of sighs.

Cempoala

The bus station is one room with a counter tended by a dark-haired young woman in a brown blazer who tells me there's no guardequipaje but maybe I could try the hotel across the street, which rents by the hour.

"If you're back after six, you'll have to pay for the night," the owner says, handing me a starchy pink towel, a roll of toilet paper, and a small bar of rose-scented soap.

A man and woman wait in the doorway, she in a denim miniskirt, he with a mustache and a collared shirt unbuttoned almost to his navel. The room smells like bleach. The toilet is offset by a partial wall made of cinderblock and painted cornflower blue. No toilet seat. I am afraid to touch anything.

Quiahuitzlán

Lugar de la lluvia where Totonac gravesites overlook the Gulf of Mexico.
The bus dropped me at a dirt road. A skinny boy tended a goat.
I climbed the mountain in sundress and sandals.
I put my hand on a rock and spread my fingers wide. The graves must have been here when she stood on this hill.
I sat on the grass, my back against a tomb, and looked out at the Gulf, the ocean that brought him, brought them. Breathe deep. Cough. Breathe deep.
Bus back to Cempoala. The driver pulls to a stop on the side of the highway at a house with a cardboard sign advertising Jugo de Noni Tahití. A woman walks toward the bus holding a baggie of juice and a straw. She and the driver smile at each other. Before she reaches his window, he puts the bus in park, gets out, and follows her into the house. He comes out twenty minutes later.

Cempoala

I arrive at dusk as the park is closing. The sun sets as I walk the ball court. The Spaniards fought each other here in 1520. Cortés and his Chinantec allies defeated Pánfilo de Narváez, who'd been sent by Diego Velázquez de Cuellar to regain control of Cortés's expedition. Narváez took a pike to the eye and was captured. Cempoala's ruler, Xicomecoatl, was wounded by Narváez's men. He survived. He was one of the first rulers to ally with Cortés agains the Mexica.

Things they didn't know: Some of Narváez's soldiers were infected with smallpox. They infected Cortés's men, who carried it back to Tenochtitlán.

Walk back through town to the bus station. Temple behind chain link, next to a tiendita. Children pass in their school uniforms, eating Takis and dulces, smacking gum.

Fiesta in the zocalo. I don't know the occasion, but I'm grateful for the families, the little ones clustered around ring toss and duck pond booths, the puestos selling everything from hot cakes to burgers to elotes. Dinner is fried plátanos con crema.

It's past six by the time I retrieve my bags. I pay the overnight fee and walk across the street to catch the bus.

Xalapa

A taxista drives me through fog in Xico Viejo.

I send a lonely email to a poet.

Tlaxcala
Murals of Xicoténcatl

A guide invites me to join a tour he's giving to a group of elementary school kids on a field trip.

The wailing woman squats beneath Quetzalcóatl, her white hair a crown of thorns, her skin ashen, a child bent and lifeless over her knee.

"Lloraba por las palabras de Quetzalcóatl, el dios blanco," the guide says. She killed her children rather than leave them to the men who were coming. "Ahora la conocemos como La Llorona."

My children, where will you go?

The guide turns to the children and asks, "They say we live in a patriarchal system, no?"

The students nod.

"Well, who is home with the children? The dad or the mom?"

"The mom!"
"Who talks to the teachers at school? The dad or the mom?"
"The mom."
I know how this story goes.
"The mom is in charge. Women control everything."
He points to La Malinche. "She was a powerful woman."
I want to stand in front of La Malinche, shield her from his judgment. I want to walk the murals alone. I am tired of hearing him talk.
"They didn't speak the language. She could have said anything she wanted. She wasn't a slave. She could have left."

Malinche

Her body holds blood that hasn't flowed in months, save what she pricks from her finger and sucks to know she is still alive, still her mother's child, still a woman of this land. Her blood tastes like dust and the sky after a storm. It tastes like snow melted in fire. It tastes like salt-cured fish, sweat, corn and the yellow hearts of manzanilla.
She imagines her baby born with a beard or covered in fur or with eyes made of blinding drops of sun.
He will be born on a horse with a shield across his chest.
She imagines him born holding her heart in his hands, still pulsing, and the only way she lives is to keep him close.
She talks to herbs, to trees and plant medicine. Mala mujer, strangler figs, copal, give and take, sacred firs whose branches reach out as hundreds of tiny crosses.

When we wake, there are blisters on our feet.

She is a river in the Yucatán, a volcano in Tlaxcala.
Orozco painted her as clay mound, eyes downcast to the warrior dead beneath Cortés's feet. He chiseled of stone. Malinche shaped of earth.

Malinche, you wrapped your green-eyed boy in a rebozo knotted over your heart. Each time he shifts, the knot slips higher up your chest, toward your shoulders and neck. You imagine the knot pressing against the nicho that flutters when you swallow, when you laugh. The knot slips higher. You let it.

You dream the Captain cuts your hair. He loosens your boy and carries him across an ocean to his king.

You don't want to walk anymore.

Cholula

Matanza is a massacre, a slaughter. In New Mexico, it's also the feast after the pig or sheep or goat is killed.

I don't want to talk. I want to take off my shoes and soak the stories up through my feet.

Some places never lose their susto. They are so small and the fright so great.

Bus to Mexico City

Did she love him? Did she love the man who burned the ships para no dejar huellas?

What did she ever own? What did we?

The poet doesn't answer.

Whole country moving toward Tepeyac. Pine boughs line altars in every village. Long walk or bicycle ride or motorcycle brigade or caravan or bus trip from Chiapas, from Puebla, from Sonora, from el otro lado, pesos and rosaries sewn into a pouch lining the waists of red sweatpants and black skirts. Torch-bearers run along highway shoulders. They take turns jumping down from the back of a pickup truck to jog the next leg of the virgencita's relay.

I won't make it to the Olmec heads. I have fellowship money. I have time. I don't want to be alone so long.

My grandma hated the place my grandpa was from, so they settled in Deming, the place she was from, bought a cinderblock house at the south edge of town, on a strip of land cleared of mesquite and rattlesnakes.

How do we gather the broken stones of our history? And what do we make of them?

Mexico City
12 de diciembre, 2007

Lo que me dice Rosa María cuando salgo del departamento por la Basílica: Prepárate. Vas a ver a gente bien jodida y lo único que les queda es la fe.
I expect my proximity to Our Lady of Guadalupe to trigger some ancient navigational system in my body that will guide me from the apartment through the subway and out again to the pilgrims and mariachis and priests who are sure to be with her tonight. I am nervous and trying not to be. Where is the red line, La Villa/Basílica, the outline of Guadalupe and the sloping peak of her basilica? I am afraid to ask for directions. Have to trust the bodies pressed against me to lead me to her feet.
Out of the subway tunnel: drums, hawkers, guitars, rattles, organs. The sound of cardboard scraping against sidewalk. Two men, two sheets of cardboard. One crawls across while the other bends and lifts the free sheet off the ground and sets it in front of the crawling man. Repeat. The crawler's heels and hands are soot black. Where did he come from?

Where did he begin? What did he promise?
Shops along the walkway sell rosaries, baptismal gowns, prayer books. Mobile vendors hawk candles, milagros, candy, and cigarettes. A light-skinned woman with wavy hair pulled back into a ponytail holds a poster board sign reading, "Peregrinos, tu meta está cerca." Next to her a tall man hands out ham and cheese tortas sealed in plastic wrap, neat as Santo Niño's satin pillow. A short woman ladles chocolate into paper cups and puts them in the hands of waiting children who reach into the crowd and exchange their gifts for a smile, a thank you. When I take my cup, I put my other hand on my heart and whisper "gracias" to the girl. She smiles and runs back to the woman for more chocolate.
Sleeping pilgrims wrapped in velvety blankets and packed tight as a tray

of rolled enchiladas line the Basílica's courtyard fences. How do they sleep with so many people, so much noise, the smells of so many bodies, of fresh roses, incense, corn, cinnamon, and dirt?

My journey here was easier than most. I follow the crowd to the moving sidewalk below the tilma. She is always beautiful, always calm, always still, no matter the spectacle around her.

I head outside and walk the gardens.

I buy a tamal de elote and ponche from a puesto halfway up the cerro. The young man handing me the tamal, still steaming through the corn husk and brown paper wrapping, says, "Eres bien guapa. Regrésate." Someday men will not say these things to me.

I sit, let the punch and tamal warm my hands, my body. I can't stay. The metro closes at midnight. But for now, I am here. She is with me. It's enough. I leave as mariachis begin to play Las Mañanitas.

You want me to say that each of us undoes the damage, finds a way to live, creates her way out of misery.

We write to heal our wounds.

A part of me dies in Mexico. Michelle the Teacher, the weeping woman. I've killed her before.

My people suffer from violence.

Drowning, casting stones—one for each fault—into water, almost hearing her thud on the sandy bottom. By fire, notebook pages, photos that lied, prescriptions, hair cut and saved in a plastic bag until the next ritual. Each time thinking it was the last. I felt I had to murder her, to scrape against a rock and lie naked beside my old skin until the new affixed itself to me.

But releasing her, this Michelle who now must rest, is easy, as easy as sweeping dried rose petals ground like bones, as sweeping the ashes of all we've burned. As easy as sinking my strong hands in red earth after the rains and before the winds of the dead, when my tierra, the land of Guadalupe/Tonantzin and Malinche is soft and ready to receive.

We are born and re-born, sister to sister, mother to daughter, Malinche to Michelle. We write to heal our wounds until we become weightless. I write a monument. I leave her, Michelle the Teacher, her image forever etched on my soul, her essence now lighter than fingerprints on black granite. I wrap her ashes in cornhusks and lay her weightless in the open earth.

Earth

donde regresa el cuerpo al silencio

After the book comes out, family calls

After all we've done for you.

After the book comes out and the phone call, my parents and I debrief

You probably didn't think about the consequences when you were writing.

After the book comes out, and I'm packing the night before going back to Oaxaca, my brother calls

I didn't want you to leave here thinking everyone hates you.

After the book comes out, and I move back from Oaxaca, and my brother owes four months of payments on the car registered in my name, my dad tries reasoning with me as he drives me to my brother's house to repossess my vehicle

Mi'ja, please don't take the car from them.

They really need it.

Mom and I can give you the money they owe. We were thinking we'd give you this car and fix up Grandpa's old one for us to drive.

Please.

Where's your compassion?

We're family. We help each other. We adjust.

> *at a stoplight*
> *turns to me*
> *sees me*

You're tired of doing all the adjusting.

> *nods*
> *takes me to my brother's*

The shittiest thing my mom ever said to me

I know you said you had to go through this by yourself, but that was your choice.

In the realm of shitty things mothers say to their daughters—which I'll know years from now when I am a stepmother and the girl I love who isn't mine comes to us pierced by her mother's words—it's not the worst thing my mother could have said. We can find our way back to each other. We do.

After the book comes out, and I move back from Oaxaca, my dad calls the week before Thanksgiving

Mi'ja, please come home.
Please.

A few days before Thanksgiving, I call my parents

Mi'ja, you are our daughter. You will always be our daughter.

After the book—years after—the other talk
brother

I was four? Maybe five. I wasn't in school yet.

It was a neighbor.

There was a group of us playing by their garage. The other boys took off on their bikes. But the older one—he was around twelve, I guess—said he wanted to show me something behind the house.

I followed him.

When he turned around, his zipper was down.

He said, "It's not fair. You can see me. I can't see you." He told me, "Pull your shorts down."

I did. He said to pull down my underwear. I didn't want to. He said he wanted to see, if I let him see, he'd let me go.

He touched me. He got my hand and put it on him.

I didn't tell anyone.

It doesn't excuse what I did to you.

Maybe that's why I'm so pissed off all the time.

My dad's words are medicine

I'm sorry you had to go through so much of this by yourself.

and my mom

I still believe in you.

She said it when I most needed it.

I still believe in you.

She spoke it after

the book, the long silence. Family take

and give, corazón cura

corazón. Yarrow stems

the bleeding. Arnica softens

the scar.

All the words spoken after the book

shards and salves

como barro con hierba de manso, pulling

out impurities, none hurt or healed like hers, my mother's.

Hers were the only words I believed.

El Ombligo

el verdadero corazón,
lo que nos conecta a la madre

"The ombligo will always lead you home."

—Jerry Tello

The Coyolxauhqui Imperative: in which Malinche's daughter gets a happy ending

Vessel:
>a craft for traveling on water.
>a hollow or concave utensil, as a cup, bowl, pitcher, or vase, used for holding liquids or other contents.
>a tube or duct, as an artery or vein, containing or conveying blood or some other body fluid.
>a duct formed in the xylem, composed of connected cells that have lost their intervening partitions, that conducts water and mineral nutrients.
>a person regarded as a holder or receiver of something, especially something nonmaterial: *a vessel of wrath; a vessel of grace.*

*

This is not the happy ending that ties up neatly with a bow. But it is an ending. And like every ending, it is also a beginning. And it is happy. It is sweet like the blue corn atole my beloved and I picked up at the Jemez Visitors Center. Before our phones were back in range. Before I knew my grandpa would not survive the weekend. Sweet like the frozen banana and berry smoothies I'd blend for my beloved's children as special treats those first hot afternoons I lived in their house, which they said was now my house, because I had no house of my own, because my apartment had been destroyed in a fire.

His daughter was seven years old. She said they'd always had extra chairs around their dining room table before I came, and how nice it was to have someone filling the empty chair now, to have four people in the house, instead of three.

Each morning she helped me pick an outfit from the rack of clothing donated to me by friends and strangers. Each morning, a skirt, a blouse, a belt, a pair of shoes, a scarf, hat, and purse. Each morning she put me together.

Henry and his children made a home for me, made it again and again.

*

Early on I tried to tell him I was broken. I showed him the pieces of me carved in stone at the base of Huitzilopochtli's temple. "You don't scare me," he said. And I knew I didn't want to scare him. I hadn't been tossed down the temple steps. I was the temple, the entrance to it, the priest at the top, a heart in my hand. I was the moon, my own light through the darkness. I was already whole. *You don't scare me.* I am not scary. I am here. I am already whole.

*

I am tall. I have hazel eyes, more brown than green, and it's only by standing close to me and really looking at my face that people notice. My first gray was a streak of silver, visible only if I parted my hair on the right. The streak is still there, but now fewer people ask if it's natural or dyed. Now strands of silver are woven throughout my hair, more than I am ready for. It's okay. I am fifty. I've helped raise two children. I've packed up one house and moved us into another, an adobe in a u-shape, with sliding doors that open onto a portal and courtyard. We've walked a girl through a rocky adolescence, a high school diploma, through boys who were wrong for her, and a car accident that totaled our Chevy Equinox but mercifully left her standing, through fights with her mother that brought her back to our house with bags stuffed tighter, then overflowing, then finally unpacked and heaped on the bed, the dresser, the floor, the hanging chair we bought in Playa del Carmen. The clerk called the chair La Princesa. We've walked a boy through the Darth Vader costume he wore to the school picnic and winter holiday showcase in pre-kinder, through eczema and scratches on the backs of his legs, through two and three in the morning wakeups because he couldn't sleep or had a bad dream or wanted one of us to lie down with him, through his sister's storms and his stillness and the afternoon he cried and cried on his bed, *I'm hungry, I'm hungry*, even though we'd just eaten, and what he was hungry for were the words to name the storm inside him. We walked him through basketball tryouts, getting the thing he wanted only to find out he didn't want it anymore. Through a school year spent at a laptop in his bedroom, jumping jacks and pushups in front of the screen, through the electric guitar he bought with his own money, teaching himself by watching YouTube, through ninth and tenth grade when hair grew over his eyes and he answered my questions with grunts and shrugs, and now he emerges, reading Dostoevsky and asking me how to write haiku.

It's taken me a long time to write this book. I tried to write from the broken place. I didn't know what to do with the broken girl, tried to fuse her together with strands of hair, spit and masa. I tossed her down the temple steps again and again, cast her head into the night sky. That head believed every bad thing, every unhappy ending, every story that ended with *you don't deserve, you're not enough, you never will, you can't.* The earth held her broken pieces. The night showed her she was light.

*

I thought I had to be perfect to deserve my beloved. I thought I had to cross the desert barefoot, holding a cup of water from which I couldn't drink.

There's a way our love heals the things inside us we couldn't reach on our own. I could have taken them to the grave, those shadows, those untended souls. But it's like when I step out of the shower, and I need lotion on the center of my back, and he knows the spot. I could live without the lotion, but it feels so good, the care, the soothing, the smell of lemon verbena or lavender.

*

The day my grandpa died, Henry walked into the hospital with me. He stood next to me as my brother stood up from the hospital cafeteria table, my brother said, "Sister," and gave me a hug. It was our first hug, our first conversation in three years. *Sister.*

I had written a book, and the book exiled me from my family. *After all we've done for you.* Or maybe I exiled myself. I didn't know how to tell my story and protect them and protect myself and put back together something I didn't break. The vessel was already cracked. My book broke it open. And maybe this book puts us back together.

*

At my grandpa's funeral the priest spoke about Grandpa's generation. These were the ones who came of age in the Great Depression, who served a country at war, some with their bodies and hearts, as my grandpa did, others by drawing lines up the backs of their legs with an eyebrow pencil, instead of a nylon seam, as my grandma did, because precious materials went to the war effort. He spoke about this generation understanding it wasn't about them. That was the day I started coming back to my family, the day I began to meld my chosen family with the family who birthed and raised and made me.

*

Henry read my book. He wrote a poem. He planted a garden. He said, "This is your home." He shared his children, stepped back enough so they could know me and I could know them. I drew stick figures on their lunch bags, read Dr. Seuss, traced their outlines on big paper and gave them crayons to color the insides. There was sorting. *Michelle's kind of our stepmom. She lives here because her apartment burned down.* Hannah Montana and a Power Ranger and Darth Vader and a piñata and Cookie Monster for Halloween. An altar every year for Día de los Muertos. I love yous freely given and then withheld and then given again, deeper, earned.

Here's what was missing.

I thought I had to be perfect.

I thought I'd have to settle. And I have; I am *settled*. We live in an adobe house. I planted sunflowers, zinnias and scarlet runner beans in the front yard bed. We have a cat, three dogs, goldfish in a pond Henry dug from the caliche in our courtyard. We had a lizard, a chicken that showed up in our yard. It's not the eagle and serpent the Mexica were promised, but it is the stuff of this home, my home, our home.

Membrane

We buried his son's   placenta   next to the peach tree he grew from pit
The peach, a gift from his father   who made orchard of the sweetest fruit
in the yard   that raised him. Chabacano   capulín   durazno de hueso pegado.
Him   a soft boy surrounded by stones.

We planted cottonwood to mark   his son's   roots. His sister
called it the gut tree   her own afterbirth feeds a locust in the mountain
house he shared   with their mother.

We patted caliche sand and clay with bare hands   filled the
cottonwood well with rain, chicken-wired the trunk to keep neighbor's
billy goat from stripping bark. As a boy
my own father butchered rabbit   painted the tree base in its blood.

I left my print in his son's gut tree loam

                                          to tell him we belong.

Notes

The following resources were essential to my understanding of Coyolxauhqui and Coatlicue:

Gloria Anzaldúa's essay, "Let Us Be the Healing of the Wound: The Coyolxauhqui Imperative—la sombra y el sueño," available in *Light in the Dark, Luz en lo Oscuro* (Duke University Press), published after Anzaldúa's death and edited by AnaLouise Keating.

The Jade Oracle: Deities & Symbols of Ancient Mexico is a gorgeous card deck meticulously researched and written by Verónica Iglesias and Anne Key, with artwork by Ramona Snow Tello, available at www.thejadeoracle.com.

"Templo Mayor at Tenochtitlan, the Coyolxauhqui Stone, and an Olmec Mask," khanacademy.org

El Museo Nacional de Antropología in Mexico City

I adapted language related to Acute Respiratory Distress Syndrome (ARDS) from the following websites:

Mayo Clinic, ARDS, symptoms & causes, https://www.mayoclinic.org/diseases-conditions/ards/symptoms-causes/syc-20355576

National Library of Medicine, National Center for Biotechnology Information, Acute Respiratory Distress Syndrome, https://www.ncbi.nlm.nih.gov/books/NBK436002/

Wikipedia, Acute Respiratory Distress Syndrome, https://en.wikipedia.org/wiki/Acute_respiratory_distress_syndrome

Acknowledgements

Thank you to the editors of the following publications in which versions of these essays and poems first appeared:

Elbow Room: "Back in critical care with pneumonia…", "…Grandma catches Grandpa slouching", "Grandma China wants me to have a husband and kids before she dies…", "Last morning of the family reunion…", "Our last conversation", "When I tell Grandma I broke up with Bad Boyfriend…", "When I tell Grandma I broke up with the Chicano attorney…" [as "The Grandma Poems"]

Great River Review: "Herencia", "Soy Yo"

Huizache: "Variations on the Death of Coyolxauhqui"

La Tolteca: "And the World Tasted of Dust"

Palabra: "Callus"

Plume: "Membrane"

Shadowbox: "Crecencio y Lute", "Casiano y Susi"

Shenandoah: "Remedio"

South Shore Review: "Sweatpants"

A special thank you to Francisco Aragón, Momotombo Press, and the Institute for Latino Studies at University of Notre Dame for publishing my chapbook *Malinche's Daughter*, without which there would be no *Vessels*, and in which earlier versions of the following essays appeared: "Mamá Malinche", "Moving Pictures", "Malinche's Daughter", "You want me to say that each of us undoes the damage…" [as "Epilogue"].

One good thing about working on a manuscript for eighteen years is all the helpers who show up along the way. My heartfelt thanks to:

the following organizations and individuals for the gifts of time, money, and project support, both for the writing of this book and for the workshops in Oaxaca: Hedgebrook, the Fulbright Program, Arturo Sandoval and the Center of Southwest Culture, McCune Charitable Foundation, Barbara Deming Memorial Fund, Letras Latinas and the Anderson Center, Esther Chávez Cano y Casa Amiga, La Casa del Ángel, Alessandra Galimberti Prince y La Nueva Babel, La Casa de la Mujer;

Edward Vidaurre and FlowerSong Press for providing a home for *Vessels* and for so many Latinx voices;

Carolyn Chavez for your organizational and administrative genius and for your good humor;

Beth Rourke, Frank & Stephanie Otero, Hilary Heyl & Juan Abeyta, and Aunt Rita & Uncle Chava for your spare bedrooms; Marisa Silva and Suzanne Sbarge & Rufus Cohen for providing a quiet place to write when I lost mine; and Apryl & Notah Begay for letting me care for your house and this story while you were out of the country;

Donna Snyder and Tumblewords, Mike Mullins, Lex Williford, and Emmy Pérez for welcoming me to your workshops, classrooms, and offices all those years ago in El Paso;

Vermont College of Fine Arts, especially Sue William Silverman, Harrison Candelaria Fletcher, Karen Taylor, and Stephanie Payne for providing a home for me and my writing when I was so far from home;

Erika Casasola por tus consejos, nuestras pláticas, tu ayuda con las traducciones, y por la medicina que compartes con humildad y elegancia;

Alberto Gutierrez for checking my pocho Spanish, connecting me with our culture, and for my fab haircut;

Las Meganenas, especially Soledad Hindi, for writing and performing Río de Lágrimas and teaching me, through word and deed, the sacred directions;

my sacred circles—Harvard U-mates, the Belize women, lxs Desnudxs, Las Creativas, Sunday Salon, CFT LA 02, TIASO, EKCO, and the Love Ninjas;

Suzanne Barbezat and the Gozo writers for re-infusing my writing practice with joy;

Norma Cantú for asking about my writing each and every time you see me; Demetria Martinez for coaching me through the dark times and celebrating the light; Valerie Martinez for supporting my work on and off the page; Sandra Cisneros for creating the Macondo Writers Workshop and for pushing me to let my reader see the basement;

Shebana Coelho, for reading an early draft and gifting me a metaphor that helped me write the next draft;

Jenn Givhan and Rich Yañez for reading next-to-next-to last and next-to-last drafts with love, compassion, and a commitment to giving this story the attention and sharp eye it needed and deserved;

Anel Flores, for your beautiful cover art, for reading so many drafts, and for your friendship, generosity, the way you create community everywhere you go, and for always having snacks;

dear, dear friends who walked and danced and cried and laughed and ate chocolate and drank with me through the writing and all the life that happened along the way—Andréa Serrano, Antionette Tellez-Humble, Avi Huelskamp, Carolina Monsivaís, Desireé Enayati, Ian Esquibel, Jennifer Granquist, Jesse Szeto, Katarina Sandoval, Kevin John Fong, Joe Weston, Lauri Harbison, Luci and Michael Cedrone, Meisha Vella, Perla Jimenez Santos, Rosa María Cortés, Sheila Abdallah, Shelle Sanchez, Tricia Dawson, Victoria Curtis;

a mis hogares—Nuevo México, El Paso, la Frontera, Oaxaca;

a mis antepasados, sobre todo Florentino y Genevieve "China" Moran;

my extended families of tías, tíos, cousins, in-laws, nieces, and nephews for all the stories we've shared around a kitchen table;

my brothers for teaching me to throw a baseball, filling our childhood home with music, sharing my sense of humor, and having my back. I love you;

Mom and Dad for always supporting me. Every parent-teacher conference, every T-ball game, every high school band concert, every milestone big and small. I love you;

Paloma and Enrique, what a gift to walk with you as your stories unfold. Thank you for letting me mother you;

and for Henry, my heart. Te amo.

About the Author

Michelle Otero is the author of *Bosque: Poems* and the essay collection *Malinche's Daughter*. She served as Albuquerque Poet Laureate from 2018-2020 and co-edited the forthcoming *New Mexico Poetry Anthology 2023* and *22 Poems and a Prayer for El Paso*, a tribute to victims of the 2019 El Paso shooting and winner of a New Mexico-Arizona Book Award. A coach, community-based artist, and racial healing practitioner, she is the founder of ArteSana Creative Consulting, dedicated to creative expression and storytelling as the basis for organizational development and positive social change. Originally from Deming, New Mexico, Otero holds a BA in history from Harvard College and an MFA in creative writing from Vermont College. She is a member of the Macondo Writers Workshop.